God Reconsidered

The Promise and Peril of Process Theology

God Reconsidered

AL TRUESDALE
editor

BEACON HILL PRESS
OF KANSAS CITY

Copyright 2010
by Beacon Hill Press of Kansas City

ISBN 978-0-8341-2537-7

Cover Design: Arthur Cherry
Interior Design: Sharon Page

All Scripture quotations not otherwise designated are from the *New Revised Standard Version* (NRSV) of the Bible, copyright 1989 by the Division of Christian Education of the National Council of the Churches of Christ in the USA. All rights reserved.

Scripture marked KJV is from the King James Version of the Bible.

The following copyrighted versions of the Bible are used by permission:

The *New King James Version* (NKJV). Copyright © 1982 by Thomas Nelson, Inc. All rights reserved.

The *Holy Bible, New International Version*® (NIV®). Copyright © 1973, 1978, 1984 by International Bible Society. Used by permission of Zondervan Publishing House. All rights reserved.

Library of Congress Cataloging-in-Publication Data

God reconsidered : the promise and peril of process theology / Al Truesdale, editor.
   p. cm.
  Includes bibliographical references (p.   ).
  ISBN 978-0-8341-2537-7 (pbk.)
 1. Process theology. I. Truesdale, Albert, 1941-
 BT83.6.G63 2010
 230'.046—dc22

2010012314

Contributors

Timothy J. Crutcher, Ph.D./S.T.D.
Southern Nazarene University
Bethany, Oklahoma

Craig Keen, Ph.D.
Professor of Systematic Theology
Azusa Pacific University
Azusa, California

Nathan R. Kerr, Ph.D.
Assistant Professor of Theology and Philosophy
Trevecca Nazarene University
Nashville

Thomas Jay Oord, Ph.D.
Professor of Theology and Philosophy
Northwest Nazarene University
Nampa, Idaho

Brent Peterson, Ph.D.
Professor of Theology
Northwest Nazarene University
Nampa, Idaho

Samuel Powell, Ph.D.
Professor of Philosophy and Theology
Point Loma Nazarene University
San Diego

Eric Severson, ABD, Boston University
Assistant Professor of Religion
Eastern Nazarene College
Quincy, Massachusetts

Al Truesdale, Ph.D.
Professor Emeritus of Philosophy of Religion and Christian Ethics
Nazarene Theology Seminary
Kansas City

John W. Wright, Ph.D.
Professor of Theology and Scripture
Point Loma Nazarene University
San Diego

Contents

Introduction	9
1. The Promise of Process Theology (Samuel Powell)	17
2. The Peril of Process Theology (Timothy J. Crutcher)	27
3. What Becomes of Revelation and the Scriptures? (John W. Wright)	39
4. What Becomes of the Triune God? (Samuel Powell)	49
5. What Becomes of Jesus Christ the Lord? (Nathan R. Kerr)	59
6. What Becomes of the Historic Creeds? (Al Truesdale)	71
7. What Becomes of the Church and Christian Discipleship? (Eric Severson)	85
8. What Becomes of Evil, Sin, Grace, and Salvation? (John W. Wright)	97
9. What Becomes of Community, the Neighbor, and the Dispossessed? (Craig Keen)	109
10. What Becomes of God's Continuing Relationship to the World (Al Truesdale)	119
11. What Becomes of the Consummation of the Kingdom of God, and Christian Hope? (Brent Peterson)	131
12. Open Theology (Timothy J. Crutcher)	143
13. A Perfect Theology Never Existed: A Rejoinder (Thomas Jay Oord)	153
Conclusion	163
Appendixes	167
Notes	181

*"Name him, Christians, name him,
With love strong as death,
name with awe and wonder
and with bated breath;
he is God the Savior, he is Christ the Lord,
ever to be worshipped,
trusted, and adored."*
(Caroline Maria Noel, 1817-77)

Introduction

Rick regretted seeing his neighbor move. "I had just gotten to know him well enough to borrow his tools!" Question the value behind Rick's statement, but he unveiled a universal human characteristic: we borrow.

We don't have tools for working or ingredients for baking? Then borrow them from a neighbor. Whole cultures borrow. Post-WWII Japan freely adopted a Western-style government and economy and then made them their own. Kings borrow. The biblical Book of First Kings tells how Solomon imported horse-drawn chariots from Egypt (1 Kings 10:26-29). Much earlier (ca. 1720 B.C.) the Egyptians "borrowed" that technology from the conquering Hyksos.

Church history shows that Christian theologians borrow. They began early. To proclaim the gospel to the Greco-Roman world, some New Testament authors borrowed concepts and tools that, strictly speaking, were not part of Jesus' ministry. To explain Jesus' relationship to God, the Gospel of John borrows and transforms a concept—*logos*—used in Hebrew poetry to personify the divine will and wisdom. The Jewish philosopher Philo (20 B.C.-A.D. 50) used the term to express the free exercise of God's energies and to reconcile Greco-Roman culture with Judaism. *Logos* also played a central role in Stoic philosophy. The apostle Paul skillfully used forms of rhetoric that were stock-in-trade for well-educated Greco-Romans. In his famous speech in Athens (Acts 17:22-31), he used knowledge of Stoic and Epicurean philosophy to proclaim the gospel.

Borrowing didn't end there. In the second century the skilled apologist Athenagoras (d. 177) liberally used the Greeks—especially Plato—to defend Christianity against its Greco-Roman accusers. Origen of Alexandria (185-232)—a Christian with a first-rate classical education—defended Christian "borrowing." He compared it to the children of Israel "plunder[ing] the Egyptians" as they hastily escaped Egyptian slavery (Exod. 3:16-22). Later, Augustine (A.D. 354-430) employed the metaphor. He said when done carefully, Christians deeply rooted in Christ can mine secular literature, science, and philosophy to better understand the faith and communicate the gospel. Tertullian of Carthage (A.D. 160-240) on the other hand opposed borrowing from Greco-Roman philosophy.

And what of the great Protestant Reformer John Calvin (1509-64)? David C. Steinmetz says that "when Calvin read the Bible, he did so, not only in company with his contemporaries and the Christian traditions that formed them, but also in an inescapable dialogue with the ancient philosophers of Athens and Rome—their wisdom, their faults, their ideas, both good and bad. . . . They . . . were as familiar and comfortable to him as the streets of his native Noyon."[1]

What about John Wesley (1703-91)—one of the principal leaders of the eighteenth-century evangelical revival? Where did this man who said, "Let me be a man of one book" (the Bible) stand with reference to "borrowing"?[2] Like Martin Luther and John Calvin before him, Wesley intended all his preaching and teaching be grounded in and governed by the Scriptures. But left alone, "a man of one book" is misleading. According to Methodist theologian Albert Outler, Wesley masterfully "understood and practiced [the] art of 'plundering the Egyptians'—their arts and letters, their philosophy and science, their political and moral insights."[3] Wesley's post-1725 reading record includes more than fourteen hundred different authors. D. Stephen Long notes that Wesley commended to Methodist preachers for their edification the works of Thomas Aquinas, John Duns Scotus, Nicolas Malebranche, and more.[4] Outler adds that not only did Wesley "plunder the Egyptians," but he encouraged us to "go and do likewise."[5]

However, a major warning is attached to Wesley's counsel. "Plundering the Egyptians" does not mean we should "remain in Egypt."[6] Even if, as Long claims, Wesley did not always succeed, he always sought to place his preaching and teaching and all he "borrowed" under scriptural governance.[7] He also was closely tutored by Christian tradition—the formative ecumenical creeds and individual theologians long revered by the church as instructive. So governed, Wesley sought "skillfully to manage"[8] the "art" of borrowing, an art he inherited from the New Testament onward.

Why do theologians borrow? They borrow to more effectively communicate the gospel to the ecclesiastical, cultural, and historical contexts in which they work. That was true of the author of John's Gospel, and it is true of the theologians who identify as "process theologians." Normally, "mission" motivates them. Schubert M. Ogden, prominent process and Methodist theologian during the latter part of the twentieth century, explains. "The theologian defaults in his responsibility if he does not make an earnest effort to state the eternal word of the Christian gospel in a way that will seem both meaningful and true to men who live in a particular time in and for which he has his theological vocation."[9]

But borrowing has its limits. If I plan to borrow my neighbor's shovel I should think about what he might expect in return. A simple "Thank you"? Or, will he accompany the shovel and tell me where to dig? How deep? Where to plant the rosebush? Might he require me to plant dogwoods instead of roses? If that were to happen, I would probably forego the shovel and consider digging with my bare hands.

The same holds true for theology. When a source outside the Christian faith—economics, psychology, or philosophy—shows promise of benefiting Christian proclamation, the conditions for "borrowing" must be carefully examined. Failure to inspect might later find us digging where and planting what we never intended. Fidelity to the Scriptures and Christian tradition excludes all "plundering of the Egyptians" that jeopardizes, or fails to enhance, fundamental Christian convictions. What will the status of the Christian faith be as expressed in the Bible and the formative, ecumenical creeds once we borrow? Who and what would the church worship and proclaim?

There is another dimension to borrowing. Have you ever borrowed and later discovered high on a shelf, or tucked in a drawer, you already owned the item you walked across the street to borrow?

As we shall see, that can happen in theology. Philosopher Charles Hartshorne charged that the dominant traditional Christian doctrine of God's perfection made him impassible (not really involved in the world, incapable of suffering or experiencing emotions). Hartshorne believed such a God to be inadequate to the picture of God the Bible offers and to our actual experience of God. To overcome the deficiency, Hartshorne offered the corrective resources of process philosophy.[10] But Christian theologians have searched other "Christian shelves" and have discovered rich resources already present in the doctrine of the Trinity that show God to be intensely active in and affected by the world. German theologian Jurgen Moltmann has done this in *The Crucified God*.[11] British theologian Colin Gunton has shown how the relational structure of human life is itself grounded in the mutual self-giving that characterizes Father, Son, and Holy Spirit.[12]

Process theologians are theologians who borrow from a school of thought known as process philosophy.[13] They think its resources can richly benefit Christian life and proclamation. This is particularly true, they say, in an era when modern physics has significantly affected our understanding of the world and human life. In harmony with the relational quality of modern physics, process philosophy explores the *developmental* and *relational* character of reality. It emphasizes *becoming* rather than *static* existence (as was characteristic of Newtonian physics). It stresses the interrelatedness of all things (entities). In fact, "to be actual is to be a process."[14] All reality—including God—is ultimately composed of *experiences* (experiential events) that have the potential to achieve novel value. This is set against the old notion that the world is composed of passive and inactive (inert) matter or substance that just endures through time. Both God and the world are seen as dynamic and intensely interactive—relational "everything affects everything else."[15]

The experiential events that constitute God and the world selectively gather up past experiential events, incorporate them into their own complex life, and "enjoy" and preserve them. Their achieved value may be incorporated into subsequent experiential events.

Instead of being distant from the world, God is essentially and uniquely *related* to it, and the world is *uniquely related* to him (all existence—God included—is essentially relational). He is "an active participant in an open-ended creative process."[16] God maximizes the potential for value in all its forms. He comprehensively experiences and values the world's moral, aesthetic, and religious beauty. Moreover, he is himself enriched by achieved value, incorporates it into his own life, and then uses it to provide goals for the world's future. Rather than coerce, God "lures the world toward new forms of realization,"[17] toward "depths of harmony" that are revelatory of God.[18] We can see that God *and* the world are in a process of becoming.

Process theologians integrate these themes into their understanding of the Christian faith. They intend to augment Christian faith and practice. For them, Scripture and Christian tradition constitute a dynamic and expanding story of varying interpretations and applications. Our appraisals of both are subject to modification if human experience and reflection require it. Christians must learn to interpret the changing shapes of tradition, creatively contribute to the process, and bravely make use of additional ways of thinking that might not have been available in the past. Process theologian Marjorie Suchocki says, "Process people think that Scripture speaks deeply about a relational world to whom and with whom God also relates. So why not use a philosophy that is relational—like Process philosophy?"[19]

When the Christian faith is understood, stated, and practiced in light of process philosophy, process theologians assure us, it becomes much richer. Long-standing deficiencies in how Christians have understood God and the world are overcome. Christian doctrine can be so stated so as to make it more comprehensible to today's Christians, more lucid for those who inquire about Christianity, and more responsive to other religions.

However, not everyone is convinced. Critics question whether process theology[20] renders faithful service to the Christian faith as its proponents claim, or whether it is best considered an alternative to apostolic Christianity. Maybe it should be judged as but another dangerous competitor tracked by church history.[21] Many observers think process theology tries to convert the Christian faith into an obedient servant of process philosophy—all the while claiming just the opposite. This volume airs some of the primary claims made in support of process theology and the charges leveled against it.

Two major proponents of process philosophy were mathematician and philosopher Alfred N. Whitehead (1861-1947) and philosopher Charles Hartshorne (1897-2000). Hartshorne went much further than Whitehead in spelling out the theological implications of process thought. He believed he was helping Christians speak more correctly and convincingly about the God whom they confess.

Daniel Day Williams (1910-73) was an early process theologian. Some more recent leaders of process theology are John B. Cobb Jr., Schubert Ogden, David Ray Griffin, and Marjorie Suchocki. The Center for Process Studies publishes *Process Studies*, a scholarly journal devoted to discussing process theology.[22]

Process theology usually takes the form of philosophical theology. This simply means that its advocates freely use philosophical concepts to frame their understanding of Christian doctrine. There is nothing inherently wrong with this. But it does entail that persons who try to explain process theology to lay readers have their work cut out for them. The contributors to this volume are working as "translators."

The ancient Greeks told of a king named Procrustes who enjoyed being hospitable to his guests. But he harbored some strange notions about hospitality. If an overnight guest was shorter than the king's bed, Procrustes would have the guest stretched to fit. If the guest was too long, the king would have his surgeon chop off all that hung over the end. Prospective guests were wise to ask in advance about Procrustes' hospitality.

The contributors to this volume examine whether process theology offers the Christian faith a Procrustean bed, or whether the "process bed" fits Christianity "to a T," as process theologians claim.

Chapter 1 explains why process theologians believe the Christian faith should appropriate process thought. Chapter 2 examines some primary components of process theology that are particularly troubling for persons committed to classical or traditional Christian faith. In Chapter 3 we will look at how Revelation and Scripture fare in the care of process theology. Chapter 4 explores what happens to the central Christian doctrine of the Trinity when submitted to process interpretation. Chapter 5 investigates how historic

Christianity's convictions regarding Jesus Christ fare under process care. Chapter 6 does the same with reference to the historic creeds. Chapter 7 examines the process account of the church and Christian discipleship. Chapter 8 asks, "What becomes of evil, sin, grace, and salvation?" when explained by process theology. Chapter 9 examines the fruit of process theology from the perspectives of community, the neighbor, and the dispossessed. Process theology makes bold claims about its treatment of God's relationship to the world. Chapter 10 examines these claims from the perspective of God's freedom, faithfulness, and grace. The New Testament says the long-awaited kingdom of God was inaugurated in Jesus' ministry, and in the Father's own timing Jesus will consummate his kingdom. Chapter 11 examines whether process theology does faithful service to Christian hope.

Open theism is a form of Christian theology that became quite attractive to many in the closing decades of the twentieth century. It continues to be an important way for understanding God's relationship to the world. It is sufficiently important and sufficiently similar to process theology to warrant distinct attention here. This happens in chapter 12.

A word of caution is in order. This book assesses the ideas and claims of process theologians as they draw upon process philosophy. The authors of the chapters might conclude that at least to some extent, process theology inadequately serves Christian faith and practice. That would be a judgment about a type of theology, not a judgment about the piety of those who embrace it.

Only the Holy Spirit knows what takes place in prayer and worship between a Christian and his or her Redeemer. A Christian might commune with and serve God in ways that rise above his or her theology or in ways that descend beneath it.

No matter how one assesses the theology that undergirds John B Cobb's *Reclaiming the Church*, his impassioned hope for renewed mission in mainline Christianity is unmistakable.[23] And Marjorie Hewitt Suchocki speaks movingly of the "touched and tasted" sacraments that "nourish" the church.[24]

We will entrust careful doctrinal examination to the trained theologians. But we will entrust examination of the heart *only* to the Holy Spirit. Together, we are engaged in faith seeking understanding. That is why Tom Oord, a respected Christian brother who has a greater appreciation for process thought than the other contributors, has been asked to provide a response.

The appendix contains a glossary of terms process theologians use. Readers not already familiar with process theology should freely consult the glossary. The appendix also contains the Nicene, Chalcedonian, Apostles', and Athanasian Creeds.

Chapter 1 Outline

Introduction

Process Theology and Science

Process Theology and the Doctrine of Creation

Questions About Theodicy

Process Theology and the Bible

Process Theology and Human Freedom

Conclusion

1
The Promise of Process Theology
Samuel Powell, Ph.D.

Introduction

Most essays in this book are critical of process theology. They are based on the assumption that this theology is not sufficiently Christian. But even if it is not, we have to account for the fact that many theologians find process theology attractive and compelling. Why is this? Let's examine five reasons. Remember, process theology is not a church that demands total belief from its members. It is a set of ideas. Anyone is free to adopt one or more of them.

Process Theology and Science

It's no secret that for the past six hundred years Christian theology has often had a rough time with science. The theory of evolution riles many Christians. But before evolution there was debate about the age of the earth and universe, and before that, unease about whether the earth lies at the center of the universe.

It's possible to exaggerate theology's tension with science—plenty of scientists have been Christians. Besides that, most Christians have made peace with science's claim that the earth is not at the center of the universe. Most accept that the earth is much more than six thousand years old.

Process theology strikes a chord with some theologians because one of its goals is to harmonize theology and science. Some Christians have a lot of sympathy for this goal while others regard modern science as a tool of the devil. They think attempts to harmonize theology with science mean rejecting God's inspired revelation. Process theology agrees with the former group. From the beginning it has been committed to achieving harmony between science and theology. So theologians who have a scientific outlook and are sympathetic to science often find process theology attractive.

We can trace process theology's affinity with science back to one of its founders, Alfred North Whitehead (1861-1947). Whitehead was a mathematician familiar with new developments in twentieth-century physics. His philosophy, which underlies process theology, was written in dialogue with those developments. Because of the scientific character of Whitehead's thought, process theologians generally believe that human understanding in all fields is dynamic and changeable, just as scientific theories change in response to new discoveries. They hold that theology should likewise be sensitive to discoveries in other disciplines, including the sciences. Theology, in other words, should be flexible and adaptive to new knowledge.

Not surprisingly, when Christians who are scientists want to dialogue with theologians, they often find it easiest to converse with process theologians. These Christians want to use scientific knowledge to help understand their faith. Many theologians influenced by other types of Christian theology have little or no interest in conversing with science. When scientists seek dialogue, the results are usually disappointing. Such theologians may be unaware of important issues or hostile toward science. This is unfortunate, because the sciences raise many important questions for Christian faith.

Process theologians promote a spirit of openness to truth wherever it is found. They believe science (as well as religion, the arts, and philosophy) is one way we learn truth. Theology has nothing to fear from and much to learn from science. Process theologians believe scientists have much to learn from religion. They strive to unify the various avenues to truth.

Process Theology and the Doctrine of Creation

As noted, process theology rests on the philosophy of Alfred North Whitehead. He was interested in creating a philosophy that combines the truths of science and religion. He was especially concerned to understand God's relation to the world. As a result, process theology has always taken a keen interest in the doctrine of creation and how God relates to the world. Many process theologians see this as a chief strength.

Why is this so notable? Isn't every theology keenly interested in the doctrine of creation and of God's relation to the world? No. All Christian theologies make some formal statement about creation. But not all theologians find the doctrine of creation critically important. Those who don't, think other doctrines are more central and deserve more attention.

If we were to survey Protestant theology through much of the twentieth century, we would see other doctrines typically crowded out the doctrine of creation. The twentieth century was marked by debates about the nature of Scripture, salvation, and Jesus Christ. These are important matters. They deserved all the attention they received. But the practical effect was that theologians had little time and energy for creation.

So, it is significant that process theology has, from its start, devoted considerable attention to the doctrine of creation. What accounts for this preoccupation with creation when many other theologies neglected it? According to process theology, the world is important to God. Doesn't every theology affirm that? After all, the Fourth Gospel tells us that God loves the world.

It's true, every Christian theology affirms the world is important to God. But process theologians point out that this affirmation doesn't agree very well with another traditional affirmation. From the beginning, Christian theologians have stated God is radically independent of the world and doesn't need the world. God created the world freely and not out of any sense of need. God was perfectly complete and blessed in eternity before creation. The world added nothing to God (since God was already perfect without it). So, although God *loves* the world, God does not *need* the world.

Process theologians say this makes God seem aloof and less than personal. It is, they argue, essential for personal beings to be involved in the lives of others. And so it is with God: God is supremely involved with others because God is intimately related to every creature—human and nonhuman. God intimately *feels* what each creature feels. This has an effect on God, just as our empathy with others has a deep effect on us. More important, God's experience of the world and of creatures in the world is an essential *part* of God. Just as I am the person I am to a large extent because of the experiences I have had, so to some extent, God is who God is because of God's experiences. They contribute to God being God.

If this is true, process theologians argue, then the traditional view of God as radically independent of the world makes no sense. God's experience is just as dependent on the world as our experience is dependent on the people and things we experience. Without them we would have no experience and hence no "existence." In the same way, without the world, God would have no concrete experience of human joy, pain, despair, and trust. God's empathy for creatures fills God's experience and enriches God's life. Without this, God would not be fully God.

Understandably, process theology has been at the forefront of environmental concerns. Because the world and its creatures are so important to God, they should be important to us as well. Preserving resources, protecting habitats, and ending environmental degradation should be very important for Christians; God has a stake in the world's well-being.

Process theology wants us to take seriously the world's importance for God. It wants us to stop thinking about God as detached and unaffected by creatures and their experiences. Finally, it wants to instill in us an ethical sensitivity so that concern for the environment becomes an important topic for theology and the church.

Questions About Theodicy

Every theology has things about which it is greatly concerned. In many cases, other types of theology show less concern about those things. Greek Orthodox theology, for instance, is passionate about saints and icons. Protestants are not.

A driving passion of process theology is theodicy. Theodicy is a theological term for the problem of evil. If God is all-good and all-powerful (omnipotent), then evil poses a problem. Why? If God is good, then God should want to eliminate evil; if God is all-powerful, God *can* eliminate evil. But evil exists. Therefore it seems that God is either not all-good or not all-powerful. In either instance, God is not God.

Discussion of this problem has a long history in Christian thought; many creative responses have been offered. Most theologians have held that although God *can* eliminate evil, God chooses not to do so. If we ask why God chooses not to eliminate evil, we find two varieties of answers: (1) in a mysterious way, evil serves God's purposes; (2) allowing evil to exist is the price God pays for creating free beings.

Process theologians object to both answers. The basic problem is that they assume God is all-powerful-able to eliminate evil but chooses not to.

The problem, process theologians say, is that the idea of an all-powerful being doesn't make sense. If God is all-powerful, then God would possess all possible power. Humans and other creatures would have no power at all. To use economic terms, power seems to be a zero-sum game: if God possesses all power, then humans possess zero. However, it seems obvious that humans do have some power—we make choices, and actions have effects. Therefore, process theologians conclude, God does not *possess* all power.

Theologians who believe that God is all-powerful think they have good answers for process theologians. In particular, they don't agree that power is a zero-sum game. However, let's follow process theologians' line of thinking. Their next step is that since God is not all-powerful, it is impossible for God to eliminate all evil. Blaming God for evil is a mistake.

Process theologians' solution to the problem of evil is a bit more involved. In their view, there are two types of power: *persuasive* and *coercive*.

We use coercive power when we try to force someone or something (pets, for example) to act contrary to their desire. Coercive power can also be called physical power. We use our bodies to move things. If I explain to a child why he or she should move away from a hot stove, I am using persuasive power. If I physically lift the child and move the child away from the stove, I am using coercive power.

Process theologians believe God possesses persuasive but not coercive power. The reason is simple: God does not have a body. Without a physical body, God is not able to move things as we do. As a result, if a comet or meteor is on a collision course with the earth, God will not be able to intervene and save the earth. If a car is bearing down on a child walking across a street, God cannot change the situation physically and save the child. None of this means God *wants* these terrible things to happen. It just means God does not have the power needed to make significant physical changes in the universe. Instead, God attempts through persuasion to move all things toward God's goals. For example, instead of physically forcing each of us to care for our neighbors, God sets before us the ideal of loving care and invites us to act accordingly. Because God uses only persuasion, God's will is frustrated when we creatures ignore persuasion and go our own way. Moreover, not only would acting coercively undercut God's character, but it would undermine human freedom and dignity as well.

Theologians who object to process theology find plenty to dislike in its theodicy. They don't like its rejection of God as omnipotent. They don't like the way process theology restricts God's action to persuasion. It is difficult, critics charge, to believe in miracles (at least big, dramatic miracles) unless you also believe that God can move physical objects around. Others object to the idea that humans can frustrate God's will. These objections are serious and deserve consideration.

At the same time, we have to give credit to process theologians for tackling a difficult subject. They have confronted a stubborn fact and tried to deal with it responsibly. There is, after all, a massive amount of evil in the world. Much evil does not seem to serve any divine purpose, and some people feel that much of it could be eliminated without damaging human freedom. If an undersea earthquake creates a tsunami killing hundreds of thousands of people, what purpose can it serve? So they ask, would our freedom really be compromised if God were to prevent the earthquake? Process theologians have an answer: Isn't it better to believe that God is simply not able to prevent such physical events?

Process Theology and the Bible

Discussion of theodicy prepares us to discuss how process theologians interpret the Bible.

Theologians have always been impressed by biblical accounts of God's actions in the world. From stories such as parting the Red Sea and Jesus' resurrection, theologians have concluded there are no limits to God's power. God's will is unstoppable and unchangeable.

But other stories in the Bible present a somewhat different picture. In Genesis, for instance, God seems to negotiate with Abraham about the destruction of Sodom. Abraham convinces God not to destroy the city if a few righteous citizens could be found (Gen. 18:16-33). Similarly, in Exodus God seems willing to be convinced by Moses not to destroy the Israelites (Exod. 32:7-14; Num. 14:10-19).

The prophetic literature also contains stories about God changing his mind, as when God decides not to destroy Nineveh once the people repented (Jon. 3:6-10). Such passages suggest God's will is not necessarily set in concrete but is flexible. They suggest God takes notice of human actions and responds appropriately. Instead of seeing God as rigidly pursuing a predetermined course of action through sheer power, they suggest God is willing to act, observe, and act again in light of human response. God's overall goal may be fixed, but God is willing to change strategy in light of human obedience or stubbornness.

The Bible's portrait of God's actions and power is thus varied. Traditional theology has focused on God's power and developed doctrines of his omnipotence and changelessness. By contrast, process theologians believe such emphases have overlooked the other way the Bible describes God—God's willingness to negotiate, to have a change of mind, and to explore alternative strategies.

Process theologians have a theory about why most theologians have ignored this other side of God: they have been influenced by a philosophical idea of God that contradicts the Bible.

Ancient Greek and Roman philosophers held that God must be (1) incapable of change, and (2) incapable of being affected by the world (impassible). In other words, God's nature was fixed and unchanging, regardless of what happens in the world. Greek and Roman philosophers thought change and the ability to be affected by things were signs of weakness and limitation. God, they felt, must be independent and fixed. God's actions and will must not depend in any way on human actions or other things in the world.

Almost all early Christian theologians accepted this view of God. Through the Middle Ages and the period of the Reformation, this was the standard Christian perception. It remains the view of many Christians.

However, process theologians believe this perception contradicts the Bible. We simply cannot find in the Bible the belief that God does not change and is unaffected by human deeds. On the contrary, process theologians believe the Bible frequently portrays God as changing and adjusting plans in response to human actions. They also emphasize that the Bible shows God suffering because of human disobedience. Think of how Hosea and Ezekiel depict God suffering as the husband of an unfaithful wife. Or think of God's anger in response to Israel's sin.

Process theologians believe they are being faithful to the Bible's picture of God when they stress God is intimately involved in the world and highly responsive to human action. A theology is needed that takes account of what the Bible teaches regarding God's relation to the world. Traditional theology is poorly suited to do this.

Process Theology and Human Freedom

A central affirmation of process theology is that God does not predestine events; God endows humans with free choice. This affirmation is one reason process theology attracts many Wesleyan theologians.

To appreciate this point it is important to understand Wesleyan theology in the Christian tradition. In Britain, Canada, and the United States, Wesleyans have always been a minority. Even if we do not include Roman Catholics, there have always been more non-Wesleyan Protestants than Wesleyans. More important, the dominant Protestant tradition in these countries has been some form of Reformed (i.e., Calvinist) theology. Wesleyans have usually found themselves in situations where the loudest Protestant voice was Calvinist.

There are many admirable features of John Calvin's theology. It has very strong, helpful, and clear views about Scripture, the Holy Spirit, the church, the sacraments, and many other subjects. However, it is also committed to a strong view of predestination. Wesleyans find two features of this position troubling: (1) God determines who will and will not be saved. God's decision to save or not to save is primarily based not on faith or lack thereof, but on God's purposes. (2) The grace by which God leads us to repentance and faith is "irresistible"; God's grace always, unfailingly accomplishes God's purposes. Grace is *causative*—it causes us to have faith.

As far back as John Wesley (1703-91), Wesleyans have objected to Calvin's understanding of predestination. There are several objections, one of which is that the doctrine of irresistible grace seriously distorts the Bible's teaching.

Wesleyans agree with Calvin that we are saved by God's grace alone and that faith and repentance are given by God. However, Wesleyans do not believe God's grace is irresistible or that God's purposes are always accomplished. On the contrary, they believe God's purposes are often frustrated because people refuse to respond positively. God's grace *enables* us to respond in repentance and faith; but it does not *compel* or *cause* obedience. Although all are touched by God's grace, many turn away and refuse to respond obediently. Wesleyans express this as *freedom*. Humans have a limited freedom to respond or not to respond to God's grace—a freedom God gives.

By now it should be obvious that process theology also affirms human freedom and responsiveness to God. It does so for various reasons, including some fairly complicated philosophical ones. Like Wesleyan theology, process theology rejects the doctrine that God predestines and that grace guarantees results. Like Wesleyan theology, it affirms that God offers grace to all and everyone can be enabled to respond positively. Not surprisingly, many Wesleyan theologians have found process theologians to be kindred spirits.

As earlier mentioned, there is an important similarity between Wesleyans' criticism of Calvin's theology and how process theologians evaluate much of traditional theology. Wesleyans believe Calvin's theology of predestination and grace ignores significant portions of the Bible. Similarly, process theologians believe traditional theology seriously misinterprets the Bible when it portrays God as incapable of change and as not being seriously affected by the world.

Wesleyans and process theologians affirm limited human freedom and believe God can empower free, obedient response. They agree that God interacts intimately with human beings. No wonder, then, some process theologians have thought that, of all the available Christian theologies, Wesleyanism lies closest to their concerns and convictions.

Conclusion

Process theology is not a flawless theology. Essays that follow will discuss some of its limitations. But every theology, including Wesleyan theology, has its limitations. Our responsibility is to separate the wheat from the chaff—to discern the truth that process theology contains and to take it seriously.

Chapter 2 Outline

Introduction

Science, Reason, and Experience

God and the World

God's Love and Power

Conclusion

2
The Peril of Process Theology
Timothy J. Crutcher, Ph.D./S.T.D.

Introduction

All theology begins in the middle of things. In order to say anything about God, one needs to assume that some things are just taken for granted. These assumptions might be deliberate and hypothetical (*"If* we say that things are like this, *then* God must be . . ."), or they might result from deep-seated intuitions ("I cannot imagine God or the world being any other way than . . ."). In either case, certain commitments are always demanded up front. This applies to process theology.

Some intuitions or commitments that ground process theology are shared by traditional Christians. Other elements look very different from ones traditional Christian faith embraces. Depending on who you talk to, that could be either an affirmation or a critique. Either way, the convictions that characterize traditional (orthodox) Christian faith provide a good place to begin assessing the *promise* and the *peril* process theology presents in the way it speaks of God and his relationship to the world.

This chapter concentrates on three fundamental aspects of process theology that are particularly problematic for traditional Christian faith. They are (1) science, reason, and experience; (2) God and the world; and (3) God's love and power. Each of these presents a peril for traditional Christian faith.

Background: Process theology begins with a particular philosophy—process philosophy—before it says anything about God or God's relationship to the world. Whenever a particular kind of theology begins by adopting a particular philosophy, it must afterward develop in a manner that complies with the underlying philosophy. The philosophical system will largely determine how the theology engages all other topics. Systematizing one's beliefs has the benefit of ferreting out contradictions between Christian theology and an underlying philosophy. When a theology relies upon a particular philosophy, it might be required to embrace things that are contrary to traditional Christian faith. The commitments are necessary for making the system work.

The *promise* of process theology comes from the way it organizes, in a coherent and often convincing way, some basic intuitions many people have about God and God's relationship to the world. This is particularly true for persons sympathetic to the Wesleyan theological tradition.

However, its *peril* arises because of what process philosophy requires of process theology. Some of the requirements conflict with classical Christian faith but are necessary for process theology to maintain its coherence; conformity with classical Christian faith would sacrifice conformity with process philosophy.

Many Christians throughout history have worked to organize their beliefs so as to get rid of contradictions. But process theology takes a big step further. It makes philosophical coherence (compliance with process philosophy) *the* controlling norm for all its efforts. This is required by two assumptions process philosophy makes about the nature of the world and God's relationship to it: (1) the importance of science, and (2) and the idea that God's nature is closely tied to the nature of the world. These assumptions are the sources for two of the three *perils*. We will explore them and then turn to the third *peril*—God's love and power.

Science, Reason, and Experience

British native Alfred North Whitehead (1861-1947) is the father of process philosophy. His ideas about the nature of the world and its bearing on the nature of God ground process philosophy. Originally a mathematician and a physicist, Whitehead turned to philosophy as a way to understand the monumental changes occurring in science during the first part of the twentieth century. His thoughts about God flow out of how he tried to understand the world.

Whitehead's insights regarding God and the world were original. They caught the attention of Charles Hartshorne (1897-2000), son of an Episcopal minister. He is usually credited with being the father of process theology.

Hartshorne was attracted to process philosophy precisely because it offered a "reasonable" or philosophical way to deal with an inescapable intuition he had about God, namely, that "God is love."[1] Like Whitehead, Hartshorne affirmed certain things about God because he believed certain things about the world. The movement from our experience of the world to making affirmations about God prepares us to see the difference between classical Christian theology and what process theology says about God.

Traditional theology is deeply rooted in beliefs about God that the church has affirmed throughout its history. Its present belief is grounded in, and justified by, what the church has historically confessed to be true. The church affirms that Scripture (the canon) informs and governs its testimony about God. Scripture is believed to be an unchanging source for truth regardless of how cultures change or science progresses. The traditional Christian does not expect to learn anything about God not already affirmed in the witness of Moses, Jesus, and Paul, as affirmed in the major creeds, and interpreted by people like Thomas Aquinas, John Calvin, and John Wesley. So strong is his or her faith in the adequacy of Scripture that traditional Christians will conclude that ideas about God that claim to be "new" cannot be "true."

Further, if the Scriptures and tradition require beliefs that cannot be fully understood or philosophically justified—such as the Trinity—then one simply accepts these things as mysteries of the faith and does not worry that they do not measure up to someone's rational standard.

Process theology does not embrace the convictions just described. Process theology—reliant upon process philosophy—presents a sustained critique of traditional Christian doctrine. Rooted in a scientific approach to the world, process theology relies much more on the tools of reason and human experience to make claims about God. It is untroubled by requirements to justify its teaching by appeal to Scripture. Though one can find scriptural quotations in the works of process thinkers such as Charles Hartshorne, John Cobb, and David Ray Griffin, their theology does not proceed from a careful examination of Scripture.[2] For process theology it is sufficient to offer good reasons for one's beliefs that derive from science, reason, and our experience of the world.

This is not to imply that traditional Christians do not care about science, reason, and experience. But they do not allow any of these to function apart from Scripture and tradition.

The foundations upon which process theology rest make it a natural theology (grounded in the world) and not a revelatory theology (grounded in revelation). A revelatory theology assumes that even though the world may teach us some things about God, knowledge of God is not primarily and naturally available in the world. Only through revelation can God be known most truly. A natural theology, on the other hand, assumes that God's nature is so closely tied to the world that we can draw adequate conclusions about him by carefully examining the world. This is why reason and experience carry such weight in process thinking, and why Scripture plays such a minor role.

As with science, for process philosophy and theology it is far more important to have experimental or experiential verification for what one believes about God than to trust what people have believed in the past—even if grounded in the Bible. So long as our belief passes the tests of observation and experimentation, so long as they hang together by these criteria, they need not be beholden to any other authority. Many of the more striking claims process theology makes flow from this vision of what is acceptable as true.

God and the World

A second peril derives from another fundamental commitment process thought requires: a close connection between the nature of God and the nature of the world. In fact, God is so deeply intertwined with the world that he can be understood only by observing the world. One of Charles Hartshorne's favorite analogies for the relationship between God and the world is that the world is the body of God. Humans are more than bodies but cannot exist without them. For process theology, God's relationship to the world is much the same. God has no being apart from the world. Originally, Hartshorne accepted the label "pantheism" to name what his analogy describes. Later he chose another term—"panentheism." Rather than saying that everything *is* God ("pan-theism"), Hartshorne claimed everything is *in* God (thus, "pan-*en*-theism"). Still, God is radically immanent. God is part of the world and does not really transcend it.[3]

Historic Christian theology rejects this. If God is truly "other" than the world, as traditional theology affirms, then we will not gain our most important knowledge of God from the world. We will know God as God makes himself known—in revelation and ultimately in the incarnation.

If God is part of the world as Hartshorne claims, we can draw accurate and adequate conclusions about him by carefully observing the world. Knowledge of God doesn't require other sources such as revelation and Scripture.

Because for process theology, knowledge of God derives from our knowledge of the world, God's role in the process system is very different from God's role in traditional or classical theology. A traditional Christian who believes that God is "other than the world," that God freely created the world and comes into it to save it from itself, is moved to worship God out of gratitude. He or she will praise God for who God is—the "One Beyond" or "Holy One," to use more traditional language. The God of traditional Christian faith can judge the world, particularly how humans respond to God's will. The response for which this God calls is far different from that of a God who is finally just part of a world that functions "naturally."

For process theology, by contrast, God explains why things are as they are in the world. God is a philosophical, explanatory principle that makes the world much more comprehensible than does the "Holy One" of traditional Christian faith. For Hartshorne, God is necessary for explaining why there is order in the world and why things in the world have value. The process God explains, justifies, and accepts this.

One can, of course, offer "praise" and "worship" to the "Originator of Order and Value" spoken of by Hartshorne, but not because God has freely done anything the world doesn't naturally require of him. What God *does*, the world requires. The process God is to be praised in recognition that God has simply fulfilled his role in the scheme of things. God has done what is "natural"—what nature requires.

But according to the Scriptures and classical Christian theology, God freely creates and redeems the world because God wants to. God's relationship to the world is "voluntary."

The process claim about God and the world shapes many other things about God. The contrast with traditional theology is acute.

Most often, traditional theology has affirmed a close connection between God and the world. But it is one that God takes on voluntarily. Traditional theology claims that God created the world "out of nothing." His nature is never to be identified or equated with the nature of the world. It is "other than the world." The world is as it is because God freely chose to make it so.

In sharp contrast, for process theology, as soon as we understand God's nature is tied to the nature of the world—God is finally part of the world—we see things could not have been any other way—either for God or for the world.

Hartshorne, for example, explicitly denies the claim that creation was "out of nothing."[4] Process theologians cannot imagine God without the world. The two are so much a part of each other they cannot be envisioned apart.

This inseparable connection between God and the world is embedded in the philosophical system upon which process theology builds. Whitehead constructed a metaphysic—a view of ultimate reality. It systematized his belief that everything is dynamic (processive) and relational. Everything—including God—is in the process of becoming. Many find this view of the world compelling and philosophically satisfying.

God's Love and Power

Process theologians use process philosophy to create a rational explanation of the Christian claim that "God is love." Their explanation directly challenges how traditional theology has understood God's love—particularly as it relates to God's power.

To understand why this is true we first need to understand two primary organizing ideas or concepts of process philosophy.

1. **Actual entities.** Whitehead believed change is fundamental to the universe. He thought of ultimate reality in a radically time-oriented way—given that changes only seem to happen "in time." He conceived of the basic units or building blocks of reality as moments of existence *in time* rather than as timeless, enduring substances. These moments, called "actual entities" or "actual occasions," are radically temporary—"drops" of existence. What we perceive as enduring objects or persons are really a series of actual occasions that follow each other in very rapid succession. Each moment is a new moment, and real change is possible at any transition between one actual occasion and the one that follows.

Each of these moments also contains a degree of freedom, a bit of choice. Of course, the level of choice for a collection of actual occasions that make up a chair, and the level of choice a person displays are very different. But at heart the same kind of freedom occurs in both. It is the freedom to be something just a little bit different—to be novel—from what came before. No actual occasion is completely determined by the ones that preceded it, and so this means reality is always changing.

Reality doesn't change *completely* from one moment to the next. The book you are reading is still the same book it was when you picked it up. And you have a sense that you are still the same person you were when you performed that action. Though Whitehead wanted to talk about reality in terms of change, he also needed to explain how things can stay the same.

2. **Prehension.** The *second* of Whitehead's structuring ideas was how actual occasions follow and relate to one another. Whitehead called the relationship of each actual occasion to the preceding one a relationship of "prehension." Hartshorne claimed this was the most important insight into reality anyone has ever had.[5] Each new actual occasion is connected to its immediate predecessor because it "remembers" that occasion and "feels" what it felt. This "feeling of the feelings" of one "actual occasion" by its successor means that although each "moment of being" is new, it is *empathetically* connected to all prior moments. The connection influences whatever freedom the new actual occasion has.

Illustration: You experience pain. Pain is a signal of distress sent by a group of cells in your body. The group of cells is what actually feels the pain if you prick yourself with a pin. However, we do not simply get a report from our cells that says, "The skin cells of the index finger of our right hand are in distress." Instead, our brain feels the feelings of those cells so strongly that it owns their experience as an experience of the whole person. We can say that we prehend the feelings of our cells so even though we are more than those cells—can even exist without them—the feelings of those specific cells shape our decisions and affect our whole person. The feelings become part of who we are.

Apply the illustration. According to Whitehead and Hartshorne, all reality results from—coheres—in process similar to what I have described. Your skin cells are not the whole of you, but their experiences certainly form a part of you. The you of the moment, when your brain registers pain, is not quite the same you that existed before pain called. Similarly, because of the influence of what you have read so far, the you that existed when you began reading this chapter is not quite the same you that you are now. Through the feeling of the feelings of the earlier you, you have a common, uniting identity called "you."

How does all this relate to love? Process theology describes "feeling the feelings of another" as love. Prehension is just another way to speak of love. Love is the thread that unites the intense interrelatedness of all things. We love ourselves by identifying with the previous version of ourselves. God loves the world in the same way; he prehends it. This is particularly true when we recall that Hartshorne's favorite analogy for the God-world relationship is that the world is the "body of God."

Understood as the process of prehension, love is the fundamental principle that holds all reality together. Traditional Christians have affirmed this from the beginning: God is love. Process theology makes love *make philosophical sense.*

But how does the process understanding of love and power create a peril for traditional Christian faith? For adherents of process philosophy the picture of actual occasions prehending their predecessors is so coherent and compelling it must be true. However, if the process vision of reality is correct, it has profound implications for how God engages the world, particularly as it relates to the kind of power God exercises.

The first implication is that given the essential similarity between God's being and our own, there are certain things God cannot do. In traditional theology, because God is Creator and "other than the world" (not part of it) the world does not limit God's power. God is, to use the traditional language, "sovereign" over the world. He is ultimately in control. God is "omnipotent," meaning there is no power God does not possess.

But for process theology, God is one actual occasion among others and the one who preserves (feels) the achieved value of all other actual occasions.

Think in terms of a single God-world system. Because the nature of the world forms God's nature, God's existence—like our own—is a process of prehending (feeling) previous moments, previous actual occasions. In fact, God feels the feelings of every actual occasion in the universe at the moment of its completion.

Now, if God is one with the world in a larger system of actual occasions that are prehending (feeling) their predecessors in time, and if God is not independent of the world, then the world will *naturally* and *necessarily* limit God's power. This happens much as the limitations of our bodies limit our power. God is necessarily dependent on the world, so he is necessarily limited by it.

In one of his later writings, Charles Hartshorne calls the doctrine of "omnipotence" a "theological mistake." He says that the traditional Christian understanding of God's omnipotence fails to recognize the radical interdependence between God and the world. Every actual occasion in the God-world system has a degree of freedom. It is the same as God's freedom, though to a lesser extent. God has some freedom to act, but his freedom is naturally and necessarily limited by the freedom everything else enjoys. God has power to influence the free choices of others, but no power to compel or coerce them. To exercise coercive power would violate the freedom of others and would undercut the very nature of reality. After all, God doesn't exist above the world; he and the world form a single reality.

Further, if God were to act coercively, he would act in an "unloving" manner. In the process system, love—which as we have seen is synonymous with prehending—and coercion are mutually exclusive. It is not just that God doesn't act forcefully, he can't. The process system excludes it.

This is at odds with traditional Christian doctrine in which God's love and sovereignty, far from being mutually exclusive, are complementary. God loves the world God freely created. God also freely accomplishes the aims of his love. The world may oppose but has absolutely no veto power over the achievement of God's purposes. The Christian faith is founded upon the conviction that in spite of all opposing powers, God powerfully fulfilled his promises in the life, death, and resurrection of Jesus Christ (2 Cor. 1:20; Eph. 1:3-14). The New Testament is absolutely certain that in God's own way and time the Kingdom he inaugurated in Jesus will be consummated (1 Cor. 15:20-28).

Conclusion

These, then, are primary commitments of a process worldview. Anyone who commits to process theology embraces them. A process theologian must be committed to a philosophical, natural, and scientific way of doing theology. What one believes about God is built upon a reasoned analysis of one's experience of, and assumptions about, the world. A traditional understanding of revelation plays no role. One must think of God as part of the same system that runs the world. God's connection to the world is natural and necessary, not freely chosen. If, as the Bible consistently claims (e.g., Ps. 33:6; 148:5-6), God were voluntarily related to the world, if the world were radically dependent upon his will, then the world would not be a trustworthy source for our statements about what the world must be like.

Finally, process theologians must be committed to a radically relational view of reality and to the limitations upon God that come with it. A process theologian must be willing to organize what he or she believes about God and the world according to Whitehead's philosophical system, not according to revelation. This will include what has been said about "actual occasions" and how they "prehend" their predecessors. It will include what we have said about an actual occasion's freedom and the limitations it places upon God's freedom. A process theologian must abandon any notion of God's power as forceful in any way, for God's freedom cannot finally infringe upon the world's freedom.

For traditional Christians, the major commitments process theology requires will be unacceptable. While there may be aspects of process theology that sound similar to traditional Christian doctrine, the similarities will be accounted for in ways radically different from what process theology offers.

Chapter 3 Outline

Introduction

Naturalistic Theism

Process Theology

What Becomes of Revelation?

What Becomes of Scripture?

Conclusion

3
What Becomes of Revelation and the Scriptures?
John W. Wright

Introduction

This chapter examines the impact of process theology upon the Christian doctrines of revelation and Scripture. But before jumping into that discussion, we need to lay a foundation.

It is no secret that the modern era has witnessed a decline in the role God plays in politics, education, law, and morality. Much of the current opposition to the church's participation in the public square would have at one time been unthinkable. Canadian philosopher Charles Taylor tracks Western culture's loss of an awareness of God. He describes the process as a loss of transcendence. Slowly, instead of seeing God as the primary source for the world and human life, Western culture began to identify the world and time as the primary location of meaning. Time (secular history), not God, has provided the direction in which the Western world looks for what is most real and important.

The meaningful and most real became immanent (located solely in the world) rather than transcendent (located in God). Instead of history gaining its meaning with reference to God, nature became the place for understanding any meaning history might have. Driving all this was the belief that what is most real—the world, life, God—can best be gained through human reason and creativity, not through God. Once this knowledge was in our grasp, it could be manipulated to bring about progress that is beneficial for everyone.

Taylor concludes that "the modern idea of order has planted us deeply and comprehensively in secular time." By their own efforts, humans can now claim to have established their own "providential social order." That order, supposedly, provides a blueprint for constructive action that can replace the "matrix of purposive forces" it was once believed God had placed in nature.[1]

I believe the philosophy Alfred North Whitehead developed in the 1920s to 1930s, known as process philosophy, is a prime example of what Taylor has described. In a radical redefinition of God contrary to the historic Christian faith, process philosophy evidences the "loss of transcendence" in Western society. It speaks the spirit of the age. Rather than championing the God of classical Christian faith, process philosophy and theology promote a "naturalistic theism."[2] The process God is arrived at by appeal to experience within nature, not to revelation, the Scriptures, and the great tradition of the church (the apostolic tradition). All that needs to be known about the process God can be gained by closely observing planet Earth through critically considered human experience.

Naturalistic Theism

What does "naturalistic theism" mean?

According to process philosophy, God is every bit as "natural" as the "world." God and the world comprise a common, natural realm in which all is "becoming," except God's primordial (eternal or abstract) nature. For process philosophy, God is "part of the furniture in the room." True, God has an "eternal" (primordial) potentiality not characteristic of the rest of the world. And true, God uniquely provides purposes for the world. But finally, God is just a different type of "enduring (continuing) object" among other "enduring objects." God is a special type of person among other persons. God functions within and is finally constrained by the same system as galaxies, solar systems, forests, rocks, caterpillars, puppies, and human beings.

Process Theology

Process theology developed on the foundations of process philosophy. It is a form of modern theology that tries to correlate Christian tradition with a given philosophical system—process philosophy. The German philosopher Immanuel Kant (1724-1804) tried something similar to this in his book *Religion Within the Limits of Reason Alone* (1793).

Basically, process theology develops independently of Christian tradition. *First,* its proponents set out to create what they see as a universal rationality to which all rational persons can subscribe. All the *primary* concepts are derived from what process philosophy supports. *Secondarily,* process theology seeks to translate a naturalistic theism (God constructed by appeal to the world) into the doctrines and language of Christian faith. But there are limits. The translation must not violate the content of the philosophical system, even if this requires significantly altering some aspects of classical Christian faith.

What is known about God by appealing to reason and experience can, with profound and often hidden modifications, be expressed in the traditional language of Christian faith. Process theologians believe that as the translation moves forward, the language of Christian tradition will enrich what can be known by reason.

Given the way mainline Protestant Christianity embraced modernity, it should not surprise us that in the 1960s many in mainline Protestant academic circles adopted process theology. It became institutionally embedded.

Taylor reminds us that the 1960s witnessed a profound moral shift in North Atlantic culture.[3] Ethics became "democratized." This sprang from an "ethic of authenticity." Self-expression and freedom spelled "self-determination" and "self-gratification," which became the central virtues. Freedom to display one's own values publicly became pivotal.

I think process theology offered a sophisticated way to legitimize and advance the moral shift Taylor describes. Process philosophy went hand-in-glove with mainline Protestantism's attempt to retain its traditional social importance, even while it was losing influence in a liberal culture now finding its meaning elsewhere (in the world itself).

Evangelical theologians developed their versions of process theology some twenty years later. Many evangelicals now wanted to influence the new culture, particularly its elite. They saw process philosophy and theology as an effective device for accomplishing this. Process theology would be a more effective and respectful way to speak evangelical faith to the new order. Supposedly, the traditional "narrow" and "peculiar" Christian language lodged in their local congregations could not accomplish this.

Trained in evangelical seminaries in the 1970s and 1980s, many evangelicals who would later embrace process theology went off to mainline Protestant institutions where process theology was influential. Interestingly, the trend was especially strong in some Methodist institutions where many Wesleyan students pursued, and continue to pursue, their doctorates.

The theology they learned often labeled itself "relational theology." The label masked the underlying (often modified) commitment to process philosophy. Having subsequently become college and seminary professors, the young doctoral graduates created process disciples. So, process philosophy and theology provided a language seminary graduates could speak in the new culture of self-sufficiency and self-determination. Supposedly, a culture that now looked to the world for meaning would understand and receive a God who could be explained within the confines of history.

For many evangelical scholars, process philosophy's naturalistic theism offered a way to participate in the newly formed secularized religious discussion in academic circles. At the same time, process theology offered a way to speak inside the church constituencies the theologians wanted to serve. But first they had to run process philosophy through traditional Christian language to make it palatable for parishioners.

Keep in mind the dual role—academic and church—of the evangelical scholars who have bought into process theology. This will be necessary for following our discussion of revelation and Scripture.

Process theologians, whether liberal or evangelical, claim their method of appropriating philosophy and the language of various cultures for articulating Christian doctrine has been used throughout Christian history. They say they are merely advancing an intellectual enterprise in which the church has regularly engaged. The Christian faith is well-served. They are correct in that there is a long history of the church appropriating thought forms to communicate the gospel.

But the claim process theologians make regarding their work fails at two very important points: revelation and the Scriptures.

What Becomes of Revelation?

In the great tradition of the Christian church, revelation disciplines reason. But the great tradition (apostolic Christian faith) regularly employs reason in the service of faith. Reason isn't annulled or abused. But revelation always governs reason, not vice versa as in process theology. The church has not merely proclaimed that God was fully present in Jesus Christ but has claimed, with the Scriptures, that Jesus was simultaneously fully human and fully God in one person. Jesus is the Salvation of the world, not just one example among others of how God acts to redeem. The New Testament and the great Christian tradition unambiguously affirm that Jesus Christ is the "Unsubstitutable One" in whom we encounter God incarnate. In Jesus of Nazareth, God definitively revealed himself and fulfilled his promises to Israel. Only revelation—not reason and not the world—can produce and substantiate this confession (Matt. 16:17).

Process philosophy doesn't belong to the order of revelation. It derives from analysis of what is confined to the world—to what we have called immanence. It belongs to a continuum—a whole—that includes God and the world. Within limits, it is true that examination of the world can aid

Christian faith. The problem with process philosophy is that it claims to have provided an adequate account of God and the world without appealing to revelation nature doesn't already provide. Though fashionable in today's intellectual climate, what process philosophy says about God excludes genuine transcendence, revelation, the testimony of the Scriptures, and the great Christian tradition.

To the extent that the process God is "transcendent" (God's primordial and consequent natures), its content always collapses back into the world. Finally, the process God does not—more correctly, cannot—rise above history and the world. History finally determines what God will be. There is no place for or need of revelation that transcends the world and history.

At best, for process philosophy "revelation" would involve God offering a prioritized list of God's aims and purpose. It would also involve using our past experiences as a provisional guide for anticipating God's future goals. But process philosophy has no place at all for a God who is quite "other" than the world even while being actively present in it.

As noted earlier, process theology presents itself as a theistic naturalism that stands between a materialistic or naturalistic understanding of the world *and* supernaturalism (the world as dependent upon God in all respects). Books that teach process theology usually begin with an introduction to Whitehead's philosophy. Then they move to a specific aspect of Christian theology where they attempt to show how process philosophy helps articulate Christian doctrine for moderns.

Sometimes process philosophy is only implicitly present as process theologians translate process concepts into language they say is faithful to the Bible and Christian theology.

At other times the influence of process philosophy is not made clear for the reader. The doctrine of revelation is a good illustration of this. Instead of beginning with what the Bible and the great Christian tradition teach about revelation and the incarnation, process theologians begin with what process philosophy permits and then apply it to Christian doctrine. As a result, process philosophy and process theologians effectively eliminate any distinction between general or universal revelation (knowledge of God communicated through ordinary experience) and special revelation (knowledge of God communicated in the life, death, and resurrection of Jesus as understood according to the Scriptures).[4]

Instead of universal revelation giving way to the primacy of special revelation, for process philosophy the opposite happens.

Nowhere is this reversal more clear than in the limitations process theology places on both the incarnation and Jesus as the Redeemer (see chapter 5). In the process schema Jesus becomes one example—perhaps the best or even an indispensable example—of what process philosophy sees as the universal meaning of revelation.

As process theologians see it, if Christians will read their Bibles correctly, they will reach conclusions about Jesus that process philosophy has gained through reason.[5] What Christian tradition really reveals is the greater truth of the emerging cosmos as described by process philosophy.

So, reason provides an accurate and controlling explanation of revelation. If Christians choose, it can be stated in terms of "revelation made known through faith." But doing so is not necessary. Donna Bowman's assessment is correct. Process thought first defines God's role in the matrix of reality and then limits what can be said about God to God's philosophically assigned role.[6]

What Becomes of Scripture?

According to the great Christian tradition, the Old and New Testaments uniquely, definitively, and authoritatively bear witness to the One God's creative and redemptive act in and through Jesus Christ.

Not so for process theology. For it, the Bible is one illustration of how God is active in all history—except for one important difference. The Bible is a record of the many different kinds of divine messages received throughout history. It is also a record of many different interpretations. This rich diversity of divine proposals offered to the world gives the Bible its authority. The Bible also contains a rich history of how diversely God's aims for the world can be interpreted.[7] Because of the Bible's rich diversity of revelation and interpretation, process theology claims, it can serve as a guide for how to receive and understand God's aims in the future. As New Testament scholar William Beardslee put it, Christians should take all biblical language seriously and treat it as offering imaginative *proposals*.[8]

The process understanding of the Bible's importance grossly misses why the Scriptures are important for the church. The Bible's importance doesn't lie in itself as a richly diverse collection of "proposals" God offers the world. Instead, it is important for the church because it bears faithful witness to the definitive, once-for-all work of God in Christ. Its importance resides in Christ whose return in glory Christians await. The risen Christ who suffered on the cross and who meets us in the breaking of the bread shapes how his followers read Scripture and seek to understand him. Christ is the treasure hidden in the field (Matt. 13:37)—in Scripture. Scripture is the treasury in which we find him. It is not the treasure itself.

Process theologians correctly insist that we should take seriously the history that lies behind a text before we can properly understand it. They are correct that we must be alert to the distinction between the historical setting of a text and how it has often been interpreted.

But they claim that to understand the Bible we must distinguish between "absolute authority" and "freedom." They say the Scriptures and Christian tradition do not have *absolute authority* for deciding what Christian faith and life should mean. Instead, process theologians say the "meaning" of Christian faith has to be worked out in a free interplay between the Scriptures, Christian tradition, and our own exploration and determination of what "Christian" means. When this happens, process theologians claim, we learn that unlike what the Bible and Christian tradition teach, Jesus is *an* "incarnation" of God, not *the* incarnation of God. Jesus manifested in his life what human life looks like when God's will is fully embraced in each situation. In important ways, Jesus reveals what God is like.

According to process theology, the interplay between "absolute authority" and "freedom" regarding the Scriptures shows us Jesus' significance; he exemplifies the divine aim that "lures" history toward a goal A. N. Whitehead and others discovered through philosophy.

Conclusion

So long as process philosophy and theology remain yoked to theistic naturalism, it cannot adequately express the Christian doctrines of revelation and therefore of Scripture. If process theology were not anchored there, it would cease to be.

Process philosophy and theology radically redefine the meaning and function of revelation and Scripture. They profoundly transform the great Christian tradition.

For process theology, revelation no longer means that God utterly and graciously overcomes the "infinite qualitative difference" between God and creation in the singular event of incarnation. According to historic Christianity, the Scriptures bear witness to the incarnation as the event in which God made possible the justification of sinners and sanctification of believers. But for process thought, revelation refers to God communicating God's eternal purpose (aim) within the confines of history. How could it be otherwise when for process theology God has no real transcendence? God is part of the God-world complex; first and finally look there.

Within the closed and naturalistic process system, revelation becomes a matter of God—part of the world—communicating how best to keep the world's future and God's future endlessly moving toward achieving values and enriching the world and God.

By contrast, for the historic faith once given to the saints, God is not "part of the world" and the world is not its own source of meaning and purpose. Its beginning, middle, and end come from outside itself—from the transcendent and eternally triune God who was made known to us in Jesus Christ.

Process theology empties revelation of God's holy and ultimate claim upon human beings. Once it has eliminated God's real transcendence, real revelation, and any real or holy distinction between God and creation, then the events in the Bible—including Jesus—become mere examples (exemplars) of what all history has experienced and valued in its own revelatory patterns. Instead of the Word made flesh (John 1:1-19), process theology delivers a God made fully present through human activity *and* divine intent.

Finally, the faith once delivered to the saints has historically *not* begun in some general notion of revelation, and then moved to the Bible and Jesus Christ. Rather, it begins and ends with the person of Jesus Christ witnessed to through the Scriptures. Christian faith is planted in this: "Christ died for our sins according to the Scriptures, . . . He was buried, and . . . He rose again the third day according to the Scriptures" (1 Cor. 15:3-4, NKJV). Knowledge of the God in whom Christians place their trust derives from the Word of God: "by Him all things were created that are in heaven and . . . on earth, visible and invisible" (Col. 1:16, NKJV), not from what reason, philosophy, or the world can support.

This is the gospel by which we will be saved, if we remain in it.

Chapter 4 Outline

Introduction

The Importance of the Doctrine of the Trinity

What Is the Christian Doctrine of the Trinity?

Process Theology's Doctrine of God

Important Differences Between Process Theology and Trinitarian Theology

Conclusion

4
What Becomes of the Triune God?
Samuel Powell, Ph.D.

Introduction

In some respects, process theology has an impressive doctrine of God. Process theologians have devoted considerable time to fine-tuning their views. They realize any theology stands or falls upon its doctrine of God. For this reason, we need to take process theology seriously. However, its doctrine of God differs significantly from the Christian doctrine of the Trinity. This doesn't necessarily mean process theology can't become "Christian," but doing so will require that it become more Trinitarian than it currently is.

Before examining process theology's doctrine of God, let's be clear about Christianity's doctrine of the Trinity. There are two important questions: (1) Why is the doctrine important? and (2) What is it about?

The Importance of the Doctrine of the Trinity

One way to grasp the importance of the Trinity is to appreciate the systematic character of Christian theology. "Systematic" means each Christian doctrine is part of an interconnected web of doctrines. A disturbance on one strand creates waves throughout. Or, it is like a mechanical engine: if one part breaks down, then the entire engine may fail or at least work improperly.

Here's an example: sanctification is the restoration of the moral image of God. So it presupposes the doctrine of the image of God. The image of God is part of the doctrine of creation. The doctrine of sanctification depends on the doctrine of creation. It also depends on Christology—the doctrine of Christ—because Jesus Christ, who is the perfect image of God, restores us in God's image. At the same time, the doctrines of creation and Christology depend on the doctrine of God, and so on. The doctrine of the Trinity provides essential support for all other doctrines. If a church ignores this doctrine or fails to appreciate its truth, its teaching will be significantly weakened in every area.

What Is the Christian Doctrine of the Trinity?

First, let's explain what the church does *not* mean by the doctrine of the Trinity.

1. The doctrine of the Trinity is not a puzzle about numbers. It is not a riddle about how three can be one. The physical illustrations of the Trinity people often use—the yolk, white, and shell of an egg, or water in the form of ice, liquid, and steam—are misguided. They assume the main thing is how something can be three and one at the same time. Those who use such illustrations forget God is transcendent. Ideas that help us understand things in the universe—space, time, and number—apply only to the created universe, not to God. Number is meaningless when applied to God.

2. The doctrine of the Trinity is not belief in three divine beings living in heaven, each with separate personality, intellect, and will. Such a belief amounts to *tritheism*—three gods. In whatever way we think of Father, Son, and Spirit, we must not compromise God's unity. Although it is important to distinguish Father, Son, and Spirit, the distinction exists within the undivided being of God.

3. The doctrine of the Trinity is often portrayed in the following highly misleading way: God is incomprehensible and cannot in any way be understood by us. However, God has revealed in the Bible that God is a Trinity. Therefore we are required to believe this because it is a revealed fact. Several problems attach to this way of portraying the doctrine. For one, it sees the Bible as a collection of mysterious truths God for some reason decided to reveal to us. But the Bible is not an encyclopedia of mysterious truths; it is a faithful witness to God's revelation (self-disclosure) as it has unfolded in the history of God's people. Second, the error portrays faith as belief in something incomprehensible that must be believed just because it is written in a book (or is authorized by the church). But the New Testament never describes faith in this way. Speaking this way separates faith from the Christian experience of salvation and the New Testament's witness to Jesus Christ.

Second, let's explain what the church does mean by the doctrine of the Trinity.

It is the church's affirmation that:

1. God is a unity and there is only one divine being (monotheism). (As noted above, we have to be careful about ascribing a number to God.) The church inherited this conviction from its Jewish heritage and has never compromised it.

2. Jesus Christ is fully divine. He is not some lesser god created by God. What it means to be God is fully present in Jesus.

3. Jesus Christ is fully human. Jesus shares in all that is authentically human. In particular, Jesus has a human body, soul, and mind.

4. The Holy Spirit is likewise a fully divine Trinitarian person and should not be thought of as merely a divine force or power.

5. The terms *Father, Son,* and *Spirit* are not arbitrary names for the same thing. They designate divine realities that are distinct.

These affirmations begin to open the heart of the doctrine of the Trinity. When stated more completely in light of the New Testament, the doctrine can be understood as follows: Although the Trinity remains beyond our complete comprehension, the Bible and the church teach that the fullness of God has come to us in the human being Jesus Christ. Contrary to human expectation, God is able to pass over into human nature and identify with that nature, even to the extent of experiencing sin's consequences and death. And yet God is able to become human and taste death without ceasing to be God. God is not transformed into a human being (doesn't cease to be God); instead, in the person of Jesus Christ God takes human nature into union with God. As a result, the life, death, and resurrection of Jesus are real events in God's life. Jesus Christ is thus the life of God entering the world in the form of a human being. At the same time, Jesus revealed God to be his Father—and by our adoption our Father also. However, the movement of God into the world does not stop here. In the Holy Spirit God comes into the world again, leading people into repentance, faith, and sanctification. The Spirit, perfecting the work of Jesus Christ, prepares the world for the time when God will be "all in all" (1 Cor. 15:28). God, therefore, is a movement stretching from the Father, through the Son and to the Spirit, and then returning to the Father at the end of history when the created world will be restored to its Creator.

Process Theology's Doctrine of God

Let's examine the idea of God as presented by process theologians. Bear in mind that process theology is a based upon a philosophy of great complexity and subtlety. Because of space limitations, only a simplified version of its doctrine of God can be presented.

There are two main points: (1) God, like us, has subjective experiences of other beings; (2) God has always had an ideal (a goal) for the universe. The second of these is more important for process theology, but the first is significant.

First, an ideal for the universe. This means that God has an everlasting, fixed goal for the universe as a whole. God also has more particular ideals for each being. What is God's overall goal? It is a combination of two aims (intentions): diversity and unity. Both are critically important to God. God wants the universe to exhibit as much diversity as possible without chaos breaking out. As process theologians understand it, the goal lies between two extremes. On one hand, the universe could lack diversity. For example, it could be composed of beings that are all alike or that never change. Absence of diversity would produce a bland, boring universe. On the other hand, the universe could be a process of ceaseless but random change. It could contain so much diversity that no unity and pattern would appear. God wants neither of these. Instead, God wants the universe to occupy an ideal middle, to achieve an ideal harmony of diversity and unity. For particular beings God provides individualized goals that, once acted upon, will help achieve God's overall ideal goal.

Second, God's subjective experiences. God vividly experiences beings in the universe. Process theologians vigorously insist on this point because they believe traditional theology doesn't take it seriously enough. God experiences beings in the world just as we do (even though God does not have a body with sense organs). The important conclusion drawn from this is that God's experiences—in fact, God's existence as a subjective being—depend on what happens in the universe. We take this for granted in human life: who we are results from the experiences we have had. Given different experiences we would be different persons. For process theologians, the same is true of God. Events in the universe have an impact on God's experiences and being. They contribute to (they constitute) God's life.

So, on one hand, God's nature is unchanging because God is always striving to achieve the ideal and fixed goal for the universe. On the other hand, God constantly changes as God experiences the world and all the changes that occur within it.

Important Differences Between Process Theology and Trinitarian Theology

In some ways process theology and Christian (Trinitarian) theology are similar. Both believe there is one God. Both believe God is good, wise, and so on. But the differences are significant also.

First, their differing purposes. The biggest difference between process theology and Trinitarian theology is that process theology was originally devised as a philosophy; it addresses questions that are specifically philosophical. Trinitarian theology was devised in response to questions about Jesus

Christ and his relationship to God the Father. So, each responds to different questions. As a result, they are very different in fundamental ways.

The differences rest on the fact that process theology began as a philosophy and has always been interested primarily in God's relation to the universe as a whole. Christian theology acknowledges that God has a relation to the entire universe. It uses words such as *creation* and *providence* to describe this relation. But Christian theology has always been much more interested in God's relation to Israel and the church. Process theology has always been impressed by the *general* features of God's relation to the world—the universal ways God relates to every creature. Christian theology, however, has always focused on God's *particular* acts in history, especially sending Jesus Christ and giving the Holy Spirit.

None of this implies that process theologians have no interest in the church or in Jesus Christ. The point is that process theology is a philosophy. Some process theologians have been Christian; others have not. So, process theology, as such, has no commitment to Christian faith (although process theologians who are Christian do have this commitment). It's not hostile to Christian theology, but it does have a different agenda. Christians who are process theologians believe its philosophical agenda is compatible with Christian theological interests.

Second, subjectivity and relationality. Another important difference between the doctrines of God as presented by process theology and Trinitarian theology is that process theology sees God primarily as a *subject* (I'm using *subject* in a narrow, technical sense). In process theology God is understood primarily as a being that has experiences, just as do humans. Trinitarian theology, however, has traditionally thought of God not so much as a subject of experiences, but as one who enters history through acts of revelation, judgment, and salvation. Of course, Trinitarian theologians haven't denied that God experiences the world. That just isn't the most important thing about God. Most important is that God has come into the world to bring salvation. The difference here between Trinitarian theology and process theology is one of emphasis.

The distinction has important consequences. Both process theology and Trinitarian theology understand God to be a relational being. They hold that an essential part of God's nature (as living) is to be related to something. Because process theology sees God primarily as a subject, it holds that God's primary relation is to the universe. But Trinitarian theology speaks of God first of all in terms of the relation between the Father and the Son in the Spirit. Only secondarily does it speak of God's relation to the world. In other words, process theology sees God as a single subject who is related to other subjects in the universe. Trinitarian theology sees God's nature as intrarelational, that is, God's nature is constituted by the relation between the Father and Son in the Spirit. Although God relates to beings in the universe, this is not God's primary relation.

Third, God's relation to the world. Discussion of God's relationality leads to another divergence between process theology and Trinitarian theology. For process theology, because God is inherently relational and because God's relation is to the universe, God cannot exist without the universe. Without a relation to the universe, God would have no experience and would therefore not be a subject. God would not exist. Because God needs the world for God's own existence, process theologians hold that the universe has no beginning—it is as everlasting as God.[1] If there had been a beginning, then there would have been a time (before the universe) when God had nothing to be related to; God would not have existed. Consequently, God requires the universe and dwells in an everlasting relation to it.

By contrast, within Trinitarian theology, God does not need the world; God's inherently relational nature is fulfilled in the relation of the Father to the Son in the Spirit. God's relation to the world is free and gracious. In relating to the world, God is not moved by any need. Trinitarian theology has from the beginning affirmed that the universe is not everlasting. It had a beginning and will have an end. From the perspective of Christian theology, process theology has seriously misunderstood the nature of the created universe and God's relation to it.

Fourth, Christology. Another major distinction between process theology and Trinitarian theology involves the doctrine of Jesus Christ (Christology). In Trinitarian theology, Jesus Christ is fully divine and fully human. Jesus is fully divine by virtue of the incarnation of the eternal Son in human nature. Now, no one pretends that this doctrine is easy to explain or grasp; two thousand years of intense discussion and thought have not answered every question. Nonetheless, the church has insisted on Jesus' full divinity because of the belief that only God can truly be the Savior.

Most process theologians, however, have felt very uneasy about Trinitarian Christology. The reason lies in how process theology understands divine action. God acts in only one way. God presents to each being an ideal goal. If the response is *positive,* then God uses it in service to his grand goal for the universe. (Of course, the goal presented to each person has to be modified according to circumstances. If, for instance, God's goal for a certain person is that he or she become a graphic artist, but that person loses both arms in an accident, God has to adjust the ideal goal.) If the response is *negative*, then God continues to present the goal (or a modified version) in hopes that eventually the being will find it alluring enough to embrace. This, for process theology, is how God acts—presenting particularized goals and persistently waiting for a positive response. The one thing God cannot do is compel a response or change a physical situation. God doesn't have a physical body necessary for exerting physical causation. In the example of the would-be artist who loses both arms, God would not be able to restore them.

So, when process theologians consider Jesus Christ they bring their understanding of how God acts. Rather than thinking of Jesus as the incarnate Son, they more typically speak of Jesus as the human being who most consistently and faithfully responded to God's ideal goal. What makes Jesus to be *the Christ* is that of all humans, he alone faithfully and perfectly responded to God's will. Jesus is important mainly because he is an example for us.

This certainly preserves Jesus' humanity. But Trinitarian theologians believe it completely overlooks Jesus' divinity. For Trinitarians, saying that Jesus responded perfectly to God is not enough. It can never make him the Savior. At best, he could be a heroic martyr or saint. To be the Savior, Jesus must be the one in whom we fully encounter God—not just an outstanding human being.

Fifth, the doctrine of the church. A final difference between process theology and Trinitarian theology lies in the doctrine of the church (ecclesiology). In Trinitarian thought, the movement of God into the world is not limited to Jesus Christ. God comes into the world in the Holy Spirit. The Spirit's principal activity is to create the church as the body of Christ. The Spirit does this by awakening people, leading them to repentance, giving them faith, and sanctifying them. The Spirit also furnishes the church with gifts necessary for its life. The church has a Trinitarian structure: being in Christ as the body of Christ, the church comes to share in Jesus' relation to God the Father. This occurs as the church lives in the power of the Spirit. The church, in other words, is (from a Trinitarian perspective) more than just a collection of human beings. It is a Trinitarian reality that shares in God's Trinitarian life. Because God is a Trinity of Father, Son, and Spirit, salvation is realized in a historical, Trinitarian reality—the church. If God were not this Trinity, salvation would simply be achieved as lone individuals obeyed God; there would be no impulse toward becoming a church—a fellowship of the Spirit.

Process theology, lacking a Trinitarian doctrine of God, does not require or support a church. Many Christian theologians are attracted to process theology and are devoted members of their own churches. But they are church members because they are Christian, not because they adopt process theology. The truth is that process theology remains a highly philosophical system of thought. This is one of its strengths. But like all philosophies today, it contains no impulse toward creating a people of God. This is not a weakness for process theology when considered as a philosophy. It would be a weakness only if it attempted to be an accurate doctrine of God and salvation. The fact that it has no power to create a people of God—the church—reveals its inadequacy as Christian (Trinitarian) theology.

Conclusion

Like other philosophies, process theology has a contribution to make to Christian theology. It helps us think in creative ways about God's relation to the world, and it raises our sensitivity to environmental concerns. It has a fresh way of emphasizing Jesus' response to and obedience to God the Father. Process theology reminds us that all creaturely response to God is theologically important.

But in spite of its contributions, process theology is not a substitute for Christian theology. Although Christians should listen carefully to process theologians and gratefully receive whatever truth they offer, the church must be faithful to its own tradition of Trinitarian thought. Only Trinitarian thought can sustain the church, its ministry, and Christian life.

Chapter 5 Outline

Introduction

Into the Heart of Love

Jesus, Incarnation, and the Revelation of What God "Is Like"

What Becomes of Jesus Christ the Lord?

Conclusion

5

What Becomes of Jesus Christ the Lord?

Nathan R. Kerr, Ph.D.

Introduction

Among the most important questions we must ask of process theologians are, "What do you make of the earliest Christian confession that Jesus Christ is God incarnate and Lord of all? Can you make this confession?" In this chapter we pose these questions and probe for answers.

The First Epistle of John says, "God is love" (1 John 4:8). Though true, the affirmation can be misunderstood. The error can distort the historic Christian confession regarding Jesus Christ. To understand that "God loves me" and that "God is loving" in a way that harmonizes with classical Christian doctrine, we must see how "God is love" roots in and flows from the earliest Christian confession that "Jesus is Lord."

Claiming that Jesus Christ is God and Lord has astonishing implications. Process theology would agree that in Christ's life we encounter the definitive disclosure of God's love *for the world in general*. But the focus is much sharper; the very *life* of Jesus—his *person*—is the "self-giving way of love" we call "God." Whatever else we might mean by "God is love," for the writer of 1 John, and the earliest Christians, it was a confession of faith that sprang from a compelling recognition that Jesus Christ *himself* is to be worshipped as Lord, as God. It isn't enough to say that Jesus demonstrates that God is love.

When we ask about the meaning of "God is love," we shouldn't first ask, *"What* is the nature of God's love?" but *"Who* is the God who loves?" The first question abstractly steps away from Jesus to find an answer. The second question stays with Jesus' person. God's love is a "who," never a "what."

If love as seen in the *person* of Jesus is *who* God is, then we will discover the true sense of what it means to say "God is love" only by giving a full account of Jesus of Nazareth's *person*, as "truly divine" and "truly human." Such a full account is called Christology (what it means to say that Jesus Christ alone is Lord). Historic Christianity confesses that the *God* who is love is who we meet in the *human* Jesus.

Process theology cannot and will not commit to such a confession about the *person* of Jesus of Nazareth. For process theology, in his *person,* Jesus is not fully God. Stated differently, process theology lacks a Christology that can unambiguously confess "Jesus is Lord." That failure is process theology's most important defect. The failure reveals that process theology is not rooted in the earliest and most formative confession of the historic Christian faith.

More pointedly, process theology's way of understanding Jesus is *idolatrous*. It seduces its adherents to worship a creature, one who is finally no more than an inhabitant of this world. How does this idolatry develop?

Process theologians claim we can know *what* love is (and so *what* "God" is) before we even consider Jesus Christ. By the time they get around to talking about Jesus, process theologians—relying on process philosophy—have already figured out what "God" and "love" mean (all this without any prior reference to Jesus). What is of ultimate importance derives from their philosophy, not from God incarnate.

What process theology knows about God in advance of Jesus is in turn used to tell us who Jesus is. The obedient life, death, and resurrection of Jesus cease to be the defining points for knowing that God is love. So, who is Jesus for process theology? He is a supreme example of our own prior knowledge of God's love.

We are compelled to say that when judged by historic Christian faith, process theology is a failure—at least its Christology. For the New Testament and historic Christian doctrine, *only* as we come in praise to confess that *Jesus is Lord* will the self-giving way of God's radical love become known to us. Christ *is* "the way" (John 14:6) but also the "stone of stumbling" (1 Pet. 2:8, NKJV).

Into the Heart of Love

To say the way process theology treats Jesus leads to idolatry is quite a charge, one that must be carefully substantiated. We begin by examining how process theology explains God's love.

It rejects what the historic creeds—especially Nicaea (A.D. 325) and Chalcedon (A.D. 451)—affirm regarding Jesus' relationship to God. Process theologians say the church relied too heavily on Greek philosophy—its language and concepts. Supposedly, the reliance caused the church to err greatly. Process theologians say the language the creeds use to identify the essential relationship between Jesus and his Heavenly Father is foreign to how we speak and think. They give two reasons for their claim.

First, the traditional Greek term "substance" used in the Nicene Creed to affirm that Jesus is of "one substance with the Father" implies a static and fixed view of God. As static "substance," God is eternally "fixed" ("frozen") in isolation from a changing world. Because of this, process theologians say, God has no essential and living relation to the world. God's "nature" is that of an aloof deity that resides outside the world.

Second, they charge that by applying the term "substance" to Christ, the church made Jesus' deity as *static* (unchanging) as God the Father. As a result, divinity could not have entered into a genuine relationship or union with humanity in Jesus. Process theologians conclude that for divine *substance* to be present in Jesus, some aspect of Jesus' human nature would have to be replaced by static divine substance (nature). Thus, they say, traditional Christology as expressed in the formative Christian creeds fails. It fails because it requires a "denial of the full humanity of Jesus."[1] In this sense, it is as though classical Christian doctrine undercut its own claims regarding Jesus as "truly divine" *and* "truly human."

Having uncovered this "fatal" flaw in historic Christian doctrine, process theology moves on to correct the "error." *First,* it jettisons the old language. *Then* it conceives of Jesus as a fully human person who perfectly reveals the nature of divine reality through an intimate, codetermining relation with the world. Let's unpack what that means.

Process theology replaces the rejected notion of "substance" with "love." "Love" is the name given to the "infinite relationality" that characterizes every aspect of the world—including God and humans. Every being (or entity) in the world—including God—exists in a mutual self-determining relationship.[2] Label this intense relationship "love." It is *mutual* in that my power of self-determination is limited by my context, and by the influence others have on me. It also means I have a similar influence on others.

Mutuality is not fundamentally something we choose. It's how the world—including God—is structured. "Love" requires that we be open and responsive to the needs and desires of others. The way reality is structured requires that we fulfill those needs and desires in ways that permit the other person to be open and responsive to my needs and desires in return. Thus, this structured mutuality of love is one in which each of us successively affects what the other will become. How you and I respond to one another in the present (as affected by our pasts) will directly influence what each of us will become in the future. Mutuality is the nature of "love."

Love as defined by process theology also has *universal* importance and impact. The mutual self-determination of *each* individual being is maximized by promoting the free self-determination of *all* individuals. How I presently act will contribute to the greatest possible self-determination of the whole (understood as the totality of individual entities) in the future.

With this understanding of love in place, we can see how process theology explains the relationship between God and humans. Mutual self-determination applies to God just as it does to humans, with one exception. For God, self-determination involves a perfect knowledge of all possibilities available to humans and other entities in each situation. God also knows perfectly which present "decisions" will best contribute to the future good of all humans and the rest of the world.[3] Therefore, God's mutual self-determination is perfectly loving. God is uniquely and perfectly open to and directly receptive of the needs of every particular being. In each situation God offers a single possibility for self-determination—an "initial aim"—that, if acted upon in love, will contribute to maximizing the mutual self-determination of the whole.

God's aim is that human beings develop in such a way that their own individual, free self-determination will coincide with the greatest good for the whole. Of course, the goal is limited by what is possible for each finite individual and situation.

The next step is to understand how the process of mutual self-determination that describes humans and others applies equally to God. Through the process of mutual development, God hopes to fulfill God's maximal possibilities. As a result of the process of human and world development, God *becomes* what God is and can be *as* God in his consequent nature (see glossary).

There is a certain moral grandeur to what I have described. But it contains a huge problem. Process theology's vision of reality subjects God to the process of mutual self-determination. Indeed, as process theologian Norman Pittenger puts it, God appears and is known to us chiefly as a mode of "our own human loving."[4] The character of the world, not God's own eternal triune life, provides the basis for understanding "God is love." God is the "chief example" of what the world is at its best. God is the "highest and best" of human love.[5] God works to manage the processes of this world beneficently, and in turn maximizes God's own becoming. God is a mere inhabitant of the world—even though its chief one.

This is the idolatry in which process theology engages.

Next we need to see how the idolatry associated with God's love applies to what process theology says about Jesus—to Christology.

Jesus, Incarnation, and the Revelation of What God "Is Like"

Christology has traditionally been concerned with how the "divine" and "human" relate to one another in the life and person of Jesus of Nazareth. Process Christology is no less concerned about this. The primary intent of process theology, however, has been to state the relationship in a way that agrees with how it understands love.

Recall that for process theology, "love" is the name given to mutual self-determination between God and humanity. God "becomes" (increases as God) as a result of acting in every moment to present to humans their highest possibilities—their initial aims—for action in the here and now. If the aims (goals) are freely accepted (become their "subjective aim") and subsequently acted upon, persons will achieve maximal good for the whole world's future.

God is "revealed" to us through the possibilities God offers. But God in turn *becomes* God as the offered aims are fulfilled. What God offers as the highest goal for humans is also the highest goal for God's self.

Now we can understand what process theologians mean when they say Jesus is "fully human" and "fully divine," and that he "reveals" God and the world. According to process theology, in Jesus of Nazareth the divine "initial aim" and Jesus' "subjective aim" (what he willed for himself) perfectly coincided.[6] Jesus' own self-determination perfectly carried out the divine "initial aim" or goal God offered Jesus—so much so that the freely chosen divine aim constituted Jesus' person. Jesus' free and complete acceptance of God's aim (God's will) perfectly mirrors what God is like.[7] Jesus "reveals" God by actualizing himself in a way that maximizes the beneficial future self-determination of all. That is how God acts and what Jesus is like.

Process theology has thereby explained, to its satisfaction, how Jesus is fully divine and fully human. Supposedly, it has avoided the "problems" associated with static "substance" (Christ is of the same "substance" with the Father) and has shown how Jesus is also fully human. But its "success" is very costly, for it has created another problem. In its "explanation," process theology has denied Jesus' full deity—something orthodox Christian faith will not permit.

Historic Christian faith affirms that the life of *this* particular man, Jesus of Nazareth, *is* the very life of God. Jesus is fully human. But he has no *independent* human identity (self)—as process theology claims—over against the triune life of God incarnate in him. Jesus is fully human (one person), but as *nothing other* than the outgoing love of God—the eternally begotten Son.[8] Furthermore, the incarnation of God in Christ is inseparable from Christ's cross and resurrection. *This* human life of unbroken obedience to the will of the Father (unto death) is *raised* and worshipped as *God and Lord*. This means far more than that Jesus had no independent human identity apart from God. It means that *this* human life that leads to death on a cross *is* the eternal, outgoing love of God.

Process theology cannot make this Christian affirmation. It requires that Jesus of Nazareth be in possession of an independent, self-determining existence. Historic Christian doctrine emphasizes how *God* takes on human flesh and defines true humanity for us. But process theology speaks of incarnation as a process by which self-determining humans take God's purposes into themselves and then *create themselves* out of what God offers.[9]

Given what process theology says about Jesus, the independent human, freely and fully embracing God's ideal aim, clearly "incarnation" need not be limited to Jesus. "Incarnation" indicates that as God offers God's best "initial aims," God is present to all persons in their process of self-construction, just as God was present for Jesus. God offers "initial aims" and lures all persons to adopt and fulfill them. Jesus is an instance of this, in fact, a particularly revelatory instance. In his historical and religious context, Jesus admirably assimilated God's aims into his fully human process of self-determination. Potentially, all persons can follow Jesus' example. Not only does the process view of the incarnation deny that Jesus is singularly and eternally the Son of God, but it makes Jesus' relation to God a uniquely *human* achievement—one for us to imitate.

Process theologian Norman Pittenger could thus say that when considering the incarnation, we should think of Jesus not as the "God-man" but as "God-in-man."[10] Jesus' uniqueness is not that he is God but that he is a creature like us who actualizes, to the most perfect degree possible, the divine aim.

Process theology has extensively reinterpreted the incarnation. It denies that the incarnation was a unique *event* of God's eternal, outgoing love. Because Jesus' response to the divine aim is something all of us can and should repeat, the incarnation of God in Jesus ceases to be God's determinative and redemptive deed for all persons. Jesus fully embraced God's initial aim offered to him (to his independent person). In turn, God benefitted and increased God's own life.

Clearly, the act of Jesus' own *creaturely* self-determination (subjectively accepting God's aims for him) is distinguished from the act of divine self-determination (God subsequently increasing as a result). Although God's will and Jesus' will "coincide," they do not "concur"—do not become one person "without separation." This is what historic Christian faith, as stated for example in the Definition of the Council of Chalcedon (A.D. 451) (see appendix), requires. Unlike process theology, orthodox Christian faith neither divides the person nor confuses the two natures. Christ is in his *one person* fully human and fully divine.

Historic Christian faith has affirmed the deep mystery that Jesus Christ *is*, uniquely, in his one person the eternal Son of God. Process theology rejects this belief and thinks that nothing of importance has been lost.

Process theology also revises the meaning of Jesus' crucifixion and resurrection. No longer is Jesus' resurrection the singular, decisive act of God by which this crucified man is raised to new life and confessed to be God and Lord. Instead, "crucifixion" becomes a metaphor for how Jesus' will perfectly coincided with God's will. In turn, "resurrection" becomes a metaphor for how God now holds up Jesus' perfect obedience as a pattern for our own self-determination.

In the hands of process theology, "cross" and "resurrection" become twin metaphors for how humans can embrace and fulfill the divine aim for themselves, the world, *and* God. Incarnation, cross, and resurrection show us how God achieves God's self-determination through the process of human self-determination.

But how does process theology gain its knowledge about Jesus? Is "revelation" its source? Yes, but as reinterpreted by process theology.

Rather than Jesus being the definitive self-disclosure of God, or straightforwardly *revealing* God to us, Jesus uniquely reveals what God *is like*.[11] God *is like* the world's process of mutual self-determination named "love." Jesus exemplifies and confirms this. What he "reveals" derives not from *who* he is but from what God *is like,* or more correctly, what the world *is like*. Jesus "reveals" what we can already know by observing the world. And what Jesus "reveals" is subject to what the world permits. That, as we have seen, is idolatrous. What Jesus reveals is assessed not on the basis of *who* he is, but by criteria independent of him, but which he exemplifies. This can happen in process theology because Jesus himself is not God. He is a human being who, by his own willing, attained a unique relationship to God.

The process account of what Jesus did encourages our own self-determination. It also reinforces our prior knowledge of what God is like. When process theology has finished, the God we end up worshipping is not the God who *is* the very *life* of Jesus, but the God arrived at by examining the world.

What Becomes of Jesus Christ the Lord?

The process idolatry becomes clearer when we examine what becomes of the Christian claim that Jesus is "Christ" and "Lord."

According to process theology, Jesus reveals what God *is like*. Yet, what God *is like* turns out to be a human "supreme ideal."[12] Jesus unveils what God is like by demonstrating what human life can become when its potential is fulfilled. Norman Pittenger leaves no doubt: Jesus is "a representation of what human existence can be and is meant to be" when experienced and lived to its uttermost.[13] There you have it. Jesus reveals God by uniquely modeling what human life can achieve when lived in harmony with the ideal of mutual self-determination.

What does process theology mean when it calls Jesus "the Christ" and "Lord"?

"The Christ" is a universal ideal. Its content is determined prior to any reference to Jesus. "Christ" isn't limited to a particular *person* as the New Testament uniformly claims. He is not the *one* anointed to rule as Lord. Instead, "Christ" is first a universal *principle* everywhere and always present; "Christ" is God's "initial aim" for the world. "Christ" becomes "incarnate" as an "initial aim." This happens repeatedly and in many different forms. As process theologian John Cobb puts it, "The universal principle of life and light, creation and redemption, which is the presence of God in all things, is what we call Christ. The redemptive, creative activity of God everywhere is what the Christian discerns as Christ."[14]

Two important points follow from this. *First,* the name "Christ" simply refers to the highest initial aim God gives to all of humanity.

What might this mean? All humans experience God's initial aim. All persons initially respond—either negatively or positively. The heart of self-determination, as process theology perceives it, is: God's initiative and human response. "Christ" is the name for God's initiative. It is active everywhere, even when humans don't know it.

Jesus is called "Christ" only because he exemplifies, in a particular life, what human response to God's "initial aim" ought to be. God's "initial aim" for all human life became "incarnate" in Jesus. He showed what all human life can become. Jesus' life isn't the only "place" where "incarnation" is happening. It is occurring in some measure wherever persons own God's initial aim.

"The Christ" refers *first* to a universal principle present in all persons, but particularly "incarnate" in Jesus.[15] As a model, he is redemptive. Clearly, this leaves open the possibility, as John Cobb argues, that any other human being can in principle "incarnate" the "Christ." Gautama Buddha, for example, confirms this. There are many others.[16]

Second, Jesus' own "incarnation" of the "Christ" might be surpassed—certainly supplemented—in our religiously diverse world.

By now the results of all this are probably obvious. "Christ" is no longer a distinctively *divine* title whose meaning is exhaustively defined by the person of Jesus. John Cobb leaves no doubt: "'Christ' does not designate Jesus as such, but refers to Jesus in a particular way, namely, as the incarnation of the divine. It does not designate deity as such but refers to deity experienced as graciously incarnate in the world."[17] Clearly, for process theology, "incarnation" no longer refers to the unique act *of God* by which God became human in time. "Incarnation" is a uniquely *human* decision to accept the divine aim, a decisive moment in one's own subjective self-determination.

The process explanation of "Christ" takes us back to our own human resources and processes. *We* determine our relation to God. *We* decide whether or not—and in what measure—to incorporate "Christ" into our creative activity. Jesus *became* the Christ and Son of God by willingly "incarnating" the "Christ" in his self-actualization. We in turn possess within ourselves the ability to follow his example.

The deviation from the New Testament and historic Christian faith is striking. In the New Testament, "Christ" is the *name* the Father gives to a particular *person* who has been appointed to rule. The *name* is given to Jesus of Nazareth—this particular *man*—who by way of his cross and resurrection is victorious over the powers and principalities of this world and has been appointed to rule as *Lord* of the cosmos. Jesus' victory, as was manifested in his death on the cross, and in his resurrection, is the very triumph of God. This is how Christianity has historically confessed and worshipped Jesus as Lord.

The "Jesus" process theology presents cannot be worshipped as *Lord and God. Glory* belongs not to Jesus the Christ, but to the world process to which God and Jesus belong. The name "God" should therefore be ascribed to the whole process of divine becoming.[18] Jesus should be imitated, not worshipped. He can be thought of as an "elder brother to be emulated, or as an authority through whom we learn to think rightly of God and neighbor."[19]

For process theology, "incarnation" does not rise above or exceed our naturally given experiences and possibilities in the world. Worship of God turns out to be indistinguishable from celebrating what is best and greatest in the world. Saying that "God is worthy of worship" amounts to saying that "the world and its processes—including God—are worthy of worship."

"Worship" will mean embracing and fulfilling God's will for rich mutual self-determination. That will be the venture of love.

Conclusion

We have seen that from the ground up, process theology builds upon an idolatrous estimate of love. This is particularly apparent in how it treats Jesus. Process theology is unwilling and constitutionally unable to confess "Jesus Christ as Lord" as do the Scriptures and historic Christian faith.

The chapter has asked, "What becomes of Jesus Christ when under the care of process theology?" The answer received is that process theology cannot affirm with the Scriptures and historic Christian faith that the very *life* of Jesus—his *person*—*is*, from all eternity, the very "self-giving way of love" we call "God."

Chapter 6 Outline

Introduction

Importance of the Creeds

Substance of the Creeds

Historic Testimonies

Can Process Theology Add Its Affirmation?

Conclusion

6
What Becomes of the Historic Creeds?
Al Truesdale, Ph.D.

Introduction

One friend is a professional archivist, the other a hoarder of old magazines and newspapers. Each one "collects," but for different reasons. The archivist strategically saves what is old; it has lasting value for understanding the institution she serves. There is nothing strategic about what the hoarder collects. Rather than serving a defensible purpose, his collection holds him hostage.

The two friends are parabolic for deciding the importance of the ancient Christian creeds: (1) the Nicene Creed (A.D. 325); (2) the Definition of the Council of Chalcedon (A.D. 451); (3) the Athanasian Creed; and (4) the Apostles' Creed (see appendix).

Importance of the Creeds

Why does the church retain and treasure its creeds? Do they contain ancient clutter the church doesn't have the courage to discard? Or, are the creeds retained because they accurately remind the church of its ancient faith and of what "Christian" continues to mean? Do the creeds accurately confess the "heart-stopping, show stopping, chart-topping" event of Jesus' life, death, and resurrection?[1]

Through the centuries, the church has affirmed just that—*"Credo, I believe!"*

Substance of the Creeds

Nicaea. In A.D. 318 Arius, a gifted priest in Alexandria, began to teach that the Son is of a different nature from the Father. Since God is one, the Son—Christ—cannot be God as the Father is God. The Son is the Father's first and highest creation. The Father appointed the Son to be the creator of all other finite things and also the world's Redeemer. If he were God, the Father would have a brother, and monotheism would be compromised. The Son should not be worshipped as God is worshipped.

Arius's teachings sparked intense unrest in the church. This eventually led to the First Council of Nicaea (A.D. 325). Once the implications of Arius's teachings became clear to the gathered bishops, his cause was doomed. The theological driver behind the council was Athanasius—secretary to the bishop of Alexandria. The creed the council produced rejected Arius's teachings and affirmed the Son to be "true God, begotten not made, of one substance with the Father, through whom all things came into being. . . . Who because of us men and for our salvation came down and became incarnate. . . ."

The Nicene Creed did not end the controversy. In A.D. 381 the Council of Constantinople (the Second Ecumenical [representing the whole church] Council) reaffirmed the Creed of Nicaea and predominantly established Nicene faith as orthodox.[2] The Nicene-Constantinopolitan Creed affirms, without reservation, that the Christian faith is Trinitarian.

Chalcedon. Nicaea established the Son's deity and incarnation but didn't explain how Jesus Christ could be fully human and fully divine in one undivided person. At Chalcedon in A.D. 451 debates regarding Christ's humanity were settled. The council produced the Definition of the Council of Chalcedon (Creed of Chalcedon). It doesn't so much explain the mystery of the incarnation as affirm what is true. Our Lord is "complete in Godhead and complete in manhood, truly God and truly man." He is of "one substance with the Father as regards his Godhead, and at the same time of one substance with us as regards his manhood." Christians neither divide Christ's person nor confuse his natures.

The Apostles' Creed (ancient title "Symbol of the Apostles") is a Symbol of Faith for Roman Catholics and Protestants. In twelve "articles" the creed articulates the fundamentals of the Christian faith (the Orthodox Church honors it and accepts its teaching but sees it as a Western baptismal creed. It isn't used in Eastern Orthodox liturgy.[3]) The creed was not written by the original apostles. It probably achieved its final form in Rome or Gaul around A.D. 500.

The creed affirms God the Father to be the Maker of heaven and earth, and Jesus Christ to be the Father's only begotten Son. It confesses Jesus' virgin birth, his passion, crucifixion, and resurrection. It declares his ascension to the Father's right hand and his promised return to judge the living and the dead. Finally, the creed affirms the deity of the Holy Spirit, confesses the holy catholic [universal] church, the forgiveness of sins, the resurrection of the body, and life everlasting.

The Athanasian Creed is a summary confession of faith approved by the Roman Catholic Church. Most Protestants value it similarly. In clear agreement with Nicaea and Chalcedon, the creed confesses that orthodox Christians "worship one God in Trinity, and Trinity in Unity." They "neither confound [confuse] the Persons nor divide the Substance [God's essence]."

Those who formulated the creeds were moved by an unwavering commitment to the integrity of the gospel and to what must be affirmed for correct faith to be maintained. God alone is the Creator, and fallen creation is in need of redemption. This requires nothing less than new creation. Hence *only* the Creator God can be the Redeemer. The New Testament testifies that Jesus Christ is the world's Redeemer and that in him we encounter not some lesser being, but God in his fullness. For those reasons the New Testament and the creeds call Jesus Christ the Lord, *Kyrios,* God!

In Jesus, God has radically identified with us, yet without ceasing to be God. He took upon himself the full humanity he sought to redeem. Jesus Christ is inseparably God the Creator and God the Redeemer.

Historic Testimonies

Can what has been said about the importance of the creeds be backed up by historic testimony? Yes!

The Orthodox Church will testify. "The doctrinal definitions of an Ecumenical Council are infallible. Thus in the eyes of the Orthodox Church, the statements of faith put out by the Seven Ecumenical Councils possess, along with the Bible, an abiding and irrevocable authority."[4]

Augustine of Hippo (354-430), one of the most important figures in the development of western Christian doctrine, bears witness. Augustine was born after the Council of Nicaea and died before Chalcedon. In his sermon to catechumens Augustine affirmed the faith of Nicaea: "We believe also in His Son, that is to say, God the Father Almighty's, His Only Son, our Lord. When you hear of the Only Son of God, acknowledge Him God. For it could not be that God's Only Son should not be God. What He is, the same did He beget."[5]

Thomas Aquinas (c. 1225-74), immensely important theologian and philosopher, speaks. The faith Christians confess distinguishes them from other people who acknowledge the existence of God.[6] This means the teaching of the Christian creeds—"the articles of faith." "The doctrine of the Catholic Faith was sufficiently laid down by the Council of Nicaea: wherefore in the subsequent councils the fathers had no mind to make any additions."[7]

Martin Luther (1483-1546) bears witness. Luther called the Council of Nicaea "the holiest and most celebrated of all the councils" and "the most Christian Council."[8] He said that the Apostles' Creed "teaches us what we have received from God. The creed, therefore, gives that which you need. This is the Christian faith: to know what you must do and what has been given to you."⁹

John Calvin (1509-64) is prepared. All the councils should be "duly respected." But they must be evaluated according to the Scriptures.¹⁰ "Those ancient Councils of Nicaea, Constantinople, the first of Ephesus, Chalcedony, and the like, which were held for refuting errors, we willingly embrace, and reverence as sacred, in so far as relates to doctrines of faith, for they contain nothing but the pure and genuine interpretation of Scripture."¹¹

John Wesley (1703-91) joins in. In a letter by a "true Protestant" to an Irish Catholic, Wesley expounded the Apostles' Creed and mixed in the heart of Nicaea and Chalcedon. The "Saviour of the world" is the "proper, natural Son of God, God of God, very God of very God; and the Lord of all, having absolute, supreme universal dominion over all things." He was "made man, joining the human nature with the divine in one person." The Holy Spirit is equal with the Father and the Son, the immediate cause of all Christian holiness.¹²

Can Process Theology Add Its Affirmation?

Christian process theologians¹³ claim that process philosophy can enhance Christian doctrine and practice. They say it makes the faith more intelligible for persons informed by modern science and religious pluralism. They restate Christian beliefs but say they discard nothing of substance. So the early fathers, Augustine, Aquinas, Luther, Calvin, and Wesley will expect process theologians to affirm without reticence the definitive Christian creeds. Will they do this?

Let's query four major process theologians: Schubert Ogden, John B. Cobb Jr., David Ray Griffin, and Marjorie Hewitt Suchocki. Differences exist between the four, but taken together they generally represent Christian process theology.

There are three major themes in the creeds: **(1) God the Creator, (2) Christ the Redeemer, and (3) the hope of the resurrection.** Here is a hint of what to expect. Suchocki says the essence of the Christian faith is probably located in its continuity and capacity for change. It depends upon repeated transformation of the message that God is for us.¹⁴ Cobb believes that God's "call forward" includes submitting all Christian doctrine to criticism and new evidence.¹⁵

First, the creeds affirm that the **triune God created the world.** What does this mean? The late British theologian Colin Gunton responds: (1) The affirmation is an essential part of the church's attempt to be faithful to revelation. (2) The confession means that God created "out of nothing" (ex nihilo). The universe had a beginning in time. There was nothing outside of God upon which he was even partially dependent. God acted freely to create the world—something completely other than himself. (3) God acted purposefully; he created the world as an act of love. God meant for the world to "go somewhere" with him.[16] (4) Creation is the work of the whole Trinity—*of* the Father, *by* the Son, and *through* the Holy Spirit. Before the creation, God already was the triune One—a communion of persons existing in mutually self-giving relations. He did not "need" the world for his completion. (5) Because of the triune relationship to the world, God continues to nurture and direct it.[17]

Will process theology say "Amen!" to that? Process philosophy makes much of what God gives to the world—its primary goals (aims) and a divine lure to achieve God's purposes. Out of God's own prior harmony, God provides and orders all possibilities for the world. But if God were limited to this, he would be incomplete. He would lack "concreteness." His "existence" is essentially relational. For God to be "related," the infinite possibilities offered to the world must be "localized"—fulfilled as concretely realized world. What God experiences or "feels" in relationship depends upon what the world becomes as it utilizes the possibilities God offers.

Let's say that God "begins" with the unification or integration of all possibilities for the world. Process calls this God's *primordial nature*. But God is *subsequently* made concrete and complete after receiving and harmonizing the manifold feelings he receives from the world.[18] Process calls this God's *consequent nature*.

There never was a time when God was merely *primordial*. Possibilities don't exist unless there is a something for which they are possible.[19] There has always been a world in some form that actualized divinely offered possibilities. For God's own completion, God has always been dependent upon a world in some realized form.

How the world actualizes the aims God offers will determine not only its own present and future but also to a large extent God's present and future. God receives the completed world into his own life. So, depending upon the quality of the world's ongoing completion, God might become richer or poorer, more or less accomplished.

Think of it! The God process theology wants us to embrace as "Christian" is one for whom the meaning of his existence is largely dependent upon a contingent world he himself only conceptually precedes.

This explanation is bedrock for a process understanding of God. Because process theology holds that the world is necessarily everlasting, it cannot affirm creation from nothing. Therefore, its beliefs regarding God as Creator cannot be reconciled with *creation out of nothing* as the creeds affirm.

Second, the creeds uniformly declare that **Jesus Christ is the Redeemer of the world.** In Jesus, God became incarnate and definitively disclosed himself for all time and all persons. New Testimony scholar Richard Hays says that for the New Testament (and the creeds) "Jesus' death and resurrection is the central decisive act of God for the salvation of humankind."[20] The apostle Paul declares in Rom. 5:18 that Christ is the only Savior for the whole human race and that his atonement is sufficient for all persons. Hays is correct; in this "contingent [historical] human form, and only here" the Word of God was made known.[21]

Will process theology make this affirmation without equivocation?

Schubert Ogden will not. He affirms that Jesus Christ is Lord, but he doesn't mean what the creeds confess. The creeds affirm Christ to be God incarnate, the triune God's definitive self-disclosure. He is the Redeemer of the world. By "Lord" Ogden means something quite different. For him "Lord" means that in a single Galilean life, God made known the promise and demand of unconditional love. In Jesus' crucifixion God made clear the radical demands of love. In Jesus' resurrection God announced that when the demands of love are obeyed—death to self-contrived security—then the promise of "new creation" begins to be fulfilled. So far, this might sound orthodox enough. There is more.

True, God spoke the word of unconditional love in Jesus of Nazareth. But God has spoken the same word in many other equally important revelatory settings. Wherever persons are, God's word of unconditional love will find ways to confront them authentically, just as God spoke through Jesus. Christ being "Lord" doesn't primarily attach to his person as the creeds affirm, but to the word of unconditional love God spoke in him. Wherever God's promise and demand of love are faithfully expressed—and that means everywhere—and in whatever form, it will always be the same promise and demand as was shown to us in Jesus.[22] God's unconditional love is universal, Jesus Christ is not.

John Cobb will not. For Cobb, Jesus Christ is no more the Redeemer of the whole world than he is for Schubert Ogden. Cobb's primary interest is in the divine Logos[23] and with how the Logos is acting in human history.

According to the creeds and the Gospel of John, we speak correctly of the Christ only when speaking of his incarnation in Jesus of Nazareth. Here and here alone God has acted to redeem the world.

Cobb rejects this claim as hopelessly parochial and outdated. According to him, "Christ" is the term we apply to all instances in which the Logos becomes historically concrete. The Logos has done this in numerous religious and cultural settings. So, "Christ" refers to all historical embodiments of the Logos.

It is true that the Logos became Christ in Jesus of Nazareth. It is correct to call him Jesus Christ. But the framers of the New Testament and the creeds made the mistake of thinking that only in Jesus of Nazareth did the Logos become incarnate, become the Christ. Our modern encounter with religious pluralism has taught us better. The Logos calls us to recognize its creative presence in many different times and places. None of the religious forms in which the Logos becomes the Christ are ultimate. Cobb wants Christians to recognize that Jesus of Nazareth, though the Christ in true form, could never completely incarnate the Logos. In fact the Logos adds to its own enrichment in each successive creative embodiment.[24] The Logos is richer now than it was when concrete in first-century Palestine.

It behooves Christians to realize that Jesus as the Christ was just one instance in which "unity with the Logos at the level of conscious human existence" occurred.[25] The Logos is eternal; Jesus is not. If Christians hold on to how the creeds speak of Jesus, they will display blindness to the creative transformation God is achieving in a religiously pluralistic world.[26]

According to Cobb, here is the Christian challenge. The Logos as Christ "confronts every settled world with some novel possibility for its creative becoming."[27] We can show faithfulness to Jesus only by immersing ourselves in the secular and pluralistic consciousness where the Christ is now working. Let us avoid identifying faith with past and particularized expressions of the Logos.[28] Let us place our hope in the creative transformation the Logos/Christ is now bringing to the world.[29]

Marjorie Hewitt Suchocki will not. But this is not immediately apparent. Initially, the language she uses in *God, Christ, Church* strikes one as quite orthodox. She explains how process philosophy can satisfy the conditions for a full communication of the nature of God.[30]

But upon closer examination, Jesus is just as parochial and limited for Suchocki as he is for Ogden and Cobb. For all three, "dialing back" the universality claimed for Jesus Christ in the creeds is required for understanding how God acts creatively in many revelatory and redemptive ways.

Essential to process philosophy is the dogma that no single historical occasion or entity can definitively embody God's aim for harmony in the world. Another way to say this is that no single finite "location" (including Jesus of Nazareth) in the universe can definitively embody God's eternal purposes for the world. The process rule that the past cannot account for all possibilities in the future applies equally to Jesus of Nazareth.[31] This helps explain why Suchocki says that "in a process world, one can never posit an unambiguous knowledge of God."[32]

For God's universal aims for harmony to be achieved, they must become historically particular.[33] Jesus was one true instance in which God's aim became concrete. Jesus correctly revealed the nature of God as love,[34] and he consistently manifested the love to which God calls us.[35] But contrary to the creeds, God's self-disclosure cannot be limited to Jesus of Nazareth. God's broad creative and redemptive goals for the world are not synonymous with the person and work of Jesus. Universality as the true nature of God is locally—but not definitively—expressed in Jesus. Suchocki wants us to see that incarnation is not limited to a single person.[36] Jesus is "relative" to the many other instances in which God's nature has become concretely manifest.[37]

The world's great religions spring from a single source, namely, the depths of God's manifold harmony. No single religion could ever be normative for the many different expressions of God's harmony. Understandably, members of a religion might be so impressed by the apparently ultimate and final nature of their faith that they would treat their religion as final. They might mistakenly commend their faith as exclusive of other religions.[38] This error has traditionally characterized Christianity.

The account of Jesus' transfiguration is correct; he "shimmered with the glory of God."[39] But that is true of all religious paths that promote conformity with God's harmony. All such religions have expressed God's diverse but united life. Each path is like a constellation in God's big sky. Each one retains its beauty in God's wide unity—by the will and grace of God.[40]

The challenge: Christians should now embrace the fact that the universal quality of religion resides in God, not in any of the religions where God diversely manifests his harmony.[41] God's harmony invites a rich community of religions that form a unity in God's depths. Knowing this, we should make use of thought forms appropriate to our own day.[42] Obviously the creeds—according to process theology—can't answer this challenge.

Third, consistent with the New Testament, each of the creeds affirms the **hope of the resurrection and the universal judgment to come.** The Nicene Creed concludes: "I look for the resurrection of the dead, and the life of the world to come. Amen." The apostle Paul instructed the Christians in Rome and Corinth regarding "the redemption of our bodies" (Rom. 8:23; 1 Cor. 15:20-28) and grounded this hope in Jesus' own resurrection. The two are inseparable. "If the dead are not raised, then Christ has not been raised" and Christians are of all persons "most to be pitied" (1 Cor. 15:16, 19; see vv. 12-19).

The Christian hope of resurrection presents a special problem for process philosophy. Temporal entities—including humans—endure only so long as it takes to satisfy their aims (goals or purposes). Life is plagued by the reality of the perpetual passing away of all creaturely things. Ogden explains that as soon as life's present moment is complete, it irretrievably slips away into the past. We must come to grips with the fact that human life is subject to an unavoidable passing away that will never be recovered. The traditional Christian hope of the resurrection runs headlong into the brute fact that "all our thoughts and feelings, loves and hates, joys and sorrows, projects and causes are relentlessly carried away from us into the past."[43]

Will Christian process theologians set aside such process limitations, and unambiguously embrace the hope of the resurrection and transformation of the whole person?

Schubert Ogden will not. After physical death, what has passed away—an identifiable experiencing person—cannot be reconstituted in some future resurrection from the dead. Christians should let go of their traditional resurrection language and embrace something better. We should think of resurrection within the context of God's pure and unbounded love.

God participates fully in the existence of all his creatures. For God, the present moment doesn't vanish into the past as it does for us. Instead, it forever retains its vividness and intensity in God's perfect love and judgment. Nothing of value is ever lost. God will remember and cherish us throughout the endless ages "in all the richness of our actual being."[44] In this way God conquers the terrors and loss associated with death.[45] This makes unnecessary the resurrection of the self spoken of in the New Testament and the creeds. The traditional Christian doctrine of the resurrection, Ogden tells us, is just mistaken.[46]

Ogden admits the possibility that humans might somehow survive death and continue to exist as experiencing subjects.[47] Maybe the soul could somehow be set free from its reliance on the body to live again after physical death. But this faint possibility is far removed from Christian hope, which looks for the resurrection and transformation of the whole person, not merely the soul's immortality.

Ogden tells us that when Christians abandon the traditional doctrine of resurrection they surrender nothing essential for Christian faith. Resurrection should never be named among necessary Christian beliefs.[48] The bottom line is that Christian language about "the last things" involves the present, not some future event. Let us concentrate on God's current promises.[49]

John Cobb and David Griffin will not. They are authors of *Process Theology: An Introductory Essay*. According to them, all attempts to affirm personal life after death are difficult to formulate in a manner not shocking and profane.[50] I once heard Cobb ask, "Why should I want to live forever?" A negative answer was clear in his question and tone of voice. Christians must confront the fact that at death our conscious identity as selves irrevocably perishes, and along with the perishing go all the conditions required for personal identity. The notion that some form of creaturely existence can endure seems inherently unbelievable.[51]

Even so, Christians should recognize that nothing of importance will be lost if they jettison the traditional doctrine of resurrection. Everything essential to the Christian hope of resurrection is made secure in our confidence that in God's consequent nature, death's threat of meaninglessness is overcome. Our joys and deeds matter in God's life. God in his love preserves them. In him they pass into permanent importance for the universe. Christians should remember that they are not themselves the everlasting reality. That designation belongs to the kingdom of God alone. The distinction should be a source of hope, not despair.[52]

At first, things seem to be different for Suchocki. She affirms the hope of the resurrection and the judgment to come. The relationship she establishes between the resurrection and a final triumph over evil is inspiring.[53] Resurrection is "a mighty transition from a finite subjectivity that is alone with itself to that same [experiencing] subjectivity within the presence of God."[54] Using process philosophy to speak this way requires a "visionary" creativity that transcends accustomed process boundaries.[55]

The reason she has to work so creatively is that in process thought nothing more can be added to a "perished" (completed) subject such as resurrection would require (1 Cor. 15:35-41).[56] So the extraordinary existence of the resurrected "I" requires us to cast off from standard process moorings and explore the open seas.[57] When the exploration is complete, Suchocki can affirm that in the resurrection, materiality will fall away and be transformed (not simply abandoned as in the immortality of the soul). Resurrection is resurrection to a spiritual body.[58]

So far, Suchocki seems to be using language generally compatible with the creeds.

But then she makes a turn that significantly separates her position from the creeds. The earlier parochial limitations placed upon Jesus return to impose similar restrictions on the resurrection. To see how this happens, we must first look at the limitation Suchocki places on the doctrine of the Trinity. Then we can see how she departs from what the creeds say about the resurrection.

Suchocki says *Trinity* is a proper symbol Christians use to name God's ever-increasing infinite complexity. It helps them speak correctly about God. But when they employ this symbol they should recognize its limitations. For one thing, Trinitarian language is limited by the times in which it was formulated. *Trinity* as symbol points beyond itself to God's inexhaustible complexity. But it should not be misconstrued to mean that by its use God's own subjective complexity has been measured. God is richer than any religion's symbols.[59]

None of this should be taken to mean that Trinitarian language is false or unimportant. It just means that naming God as Trinity is conditioned by particularities other religions do not share.

Now let's see how this applies to the resurrection. Just as *Trinity* as symbol is uniquely Christian and can't serve the needs of other religions, even so *resurrection* and final judgment designate uniquely Christian expectations. Resurrection is an illustration of how God "bends" to fulfill diverse religious narratives. Christians expect the resurrection to be associated with the consummation of the kingdom of God. While this is essential for the Christian narrative, it isn't true for all religions. The creeds' expectation that the resurrection of the dead will signal the consummation of human history is simply incorrect. There is no single divine plan for the world's future now moving toward completion. Fleshing out God's outline for the future depends upon what the universe in its self-creativity will become. Far from a universal consummation of God's kingdom as the New Testament and the creeds expect, there is a novel future for God and the world. History will determine the notes that will compose the divine harmony.[60] God's future and the world's future transcend the unique expectations of Christianity.

Conclusion

We can now ask two questions: First, with which friend's "collection" would process theology most closely identify the Christian creeds? Second, would Augustine, Aquinas, Luther, Calvin, and Wesley recognize in Ogden,

Cobb, Griffin, and Suchocki good stewards of the faith they long ago proclaimed?[61]

Chapter 7 Outline

Nathan

The Appeal of Process Theology

Obstacles That Blunt the Process Appeal

    Science Comes First

    Maximizing Enjoyment

    Utilitarian Love

    The Foolishness of the Gospel

Conclusion

7

What Becomes of the Church and Christian Discipleship?

Eric Severson

Nathan

Nathan stumbled into my office, twitching and scratching at his body. He was not a member of the congregation that called me "pastor," but he had attended on Easter once or twice. Some of his extended family were members. Nathan's first words were, "I'm gonna lose my family." Stopping periodically to claw at the back of his head, he told me about his drift into methamphetamine addiction, and how his voracious and expensive habit had forced his young wife to consult a divorce lawyer. Nathan didn't really want help, but his wife's threats had driven him to our church for assistance.

As Nathan spoke, he continued to scrape and pound at the back of his skull. He was convinced that his occipital bone—the lumpy knob on the back of our heads—was a nest of spiders hatching underneath his skin. He demonstrated the common side effects of methamphetamine addiction. Nathan hadn't slept in days. His eyes looked bloodshot and hollow. He was in horrible condition.

Christian churches and clergy are often caught in difficult situations. As pastor, I was already "up to my ears" in caring for a struggling congregation. Nathan's interruption would be costly. Worse yet, his prospects for recovery seemed very poor. His past, it turned out, was riddled with failures to recover from addiction. His parents had given up. His wife was ready for divorce. By all reasonable estimates, the time, energy, and money invested in Nathan would be squandered. The "waste" would come at the expense of others. Hospitalized parishioners were waiting for their pastor's visit. Lonely senior citizens hoped I would visit them. Parishioners young and old were barely hanging on to their sanity.

Nathan's needs were extensive. Addressing them would be expensive. Many hours of attention would be required just to convince him to enter rehab. Even then, Nathan would likely repeat a pattern of expensive but futile attempts to conquer an addiction he seemed ultimately unwilling to fight.

If anyone's situation could be classified as hopeless, Nathan's seemed to qualify. He certainly didn't appear to have much hope for himself, and his "hopelessness" seemed to be justified. Chances of successfully helping Nathan were slimmer than playing the lottery. Wouldn't the costs be downright *irresponsible*? Wouldn't helping Nathan come at the cost of my congregation's greater needs? Still, in such moments should Christians calculate costs and benefits before helping others? For sincere Christians, this is no simple matter.

As a pastor seeking guidance for difficult choices, process theism (theology) seemed to offer clear and well-defined answers. Part of the "promise" of process theology is its rigorous practicality—its smooth interface between philosophy and practice.

On my office bookshelf were several helpful books written by process theologians. Of particular interest was Marjorie Suchocki's *God, Christ, Church*.[1] My own struggles to resolve the stubborn "problem of evil" had led me to her version of process theology. I found comfort in her explanation that God is already doing God's best to fix a chaotic and broken world. Suchocki calls for a church that looks for creative ways to assist God in his world-mending and world-making efforts. This would require heeding protests against injustice voiced by a suffering world.

Suchocki subtitles her book "A Practical Guide to Process Theology." The book brims with practical perspectives on how process theism and Christian faith dovetail. She is noted for her practical applications. Numerous other process authors have also discussed the intersection between process theology and Christian discipleship.[2]

Nevertheless, on the day of my discussion with Nathan I began to doubt the compatibility between Christian love and hope, and the philosophy that undergirds process theism.

Explore with me how process theism leads us to think about the Christian church and Christian discipleship. I will also evaluate the promise of process theology in light of the "foolishness" of the gospel.

The Appeal of Process Theology

Before exposing what seems to be the chief incompatibility between Christian hope and process theology, let's acknowledge its appeal. There is reason to applaud the way process theology speaks of Christian love, patience, and community. Initially, the ideals it prizes seem to be compatible with virtues commonly praised in Christian theology.

Part of process theology's appeal resides in the importance it assigns to love and harmony in the world. It seeks, and even depends on, a sweeping vision of what has been and how God will act in the future.

According to process thought, theologians should act as good scientists by analyzing the past, assessing the present, and trying to anticipate the future. Process theologians place God at the center of this responsibility. Not only does God provide each *concrescing* (the process of becoming) actual occasion with an ideal aim (purpose) for self-actualization, but God "experiences" the world and then receives that experience into God's own life as well. God reworks what he experiences and uses his creativity to promote a more harmonious world. In love, God lures or draws the world toward an ever-increasing harmony. Harmony replaces conflict with peace, pain with healing, and division with reconciliation. Maximizing, preserving, and integrating value is God's full-time activity. Who could question the merit of such activity? What Christian would not applaud God's effort to maximize the achievement of value in the world?

Obstacles That Blunt the Process Appeal

In spite of process theology's clear appeal, major obstacles challenge its compatibility with Christian theology, one of which is the divergence between how process thought speaks of God and how apostolic Christian faith has spoken of God. But the incompatibility I want to target lies elsewhere. It has to do with the church and Christian discipleship. Though at times it may appear subtly, process theology substantially departs from what Christians have traditionally meant by "church" and "discipleship."

The church plays a significant role in process theology. Process theologians John Cobb and David Ray Griffin claim that a process vision of community can correct and heal divisions in Christian churches.[3] They call for communities that function with mutual voluntary respect. "This is an appropriate vision for Christians since in its origin the church was this kind of community."[4] Suchocki uses process thought to promote a church faithful to its past and adaptable to the present so that it might secure a more genuinely Christian future. The process emphasis on harmony is notable.

Science Comes First

However, serious problems arise when process thought is applied to the church and to life in Christian community. Process theology originates in and is governed by a strong commitment to modern science. "Process thought seeks to integrate and reconcile the diverse facets of human experience (i.e., ethical, religious, aesthetic, and scientific intuitions) into one coherent explanatory scheme." It utilizes a "methodology that integrates both speculation and empirical verification."[5] A scientific understanding of the world governs what process theology says about God and the world. It does not originate in, nor is it governed by, the Scriptures and apostolic faith. That is cause for alarm. There is in process thought a kind of intoxication by science and far too little attention to the Scriptures and Christian tradition.

The importance of science is not to be discounted. All of us are indebted. From it we learn to differentiate between neutrons and electrons, edible food and poisons, hurricanes and minor storms. Given the importance of science, we should not be surprised when philosophers and theologians take the sciences seriously. Process theologians work to bridge science and religion and to show the importance of science for Christian faith and living.

But as legitimate as this impulse is in many instances, it harbors a major danger for understanding the church and Christian life. The church and Christian faith are fundamentally *rooted in* and *defined by* a "foolishness" that can never be reconciled with scientific expectations, processes, values, and precision. What the church and Christian life are all about is unthinkable when submitted to scientific reasoning. To be "church" and "Christian" entails putting one's trust in what scientific precision and logic would label "questionable causes."

This doesn't mean that Christians should jettison careful thought. But it does mean that when we follow the gospel of Jesus Christ we walk in a direction scientific precision cannot endorse. The "foolishness" of Christian hope travels a different path. We abandon the logic of precision, of "what makes sense," and of what can be empirically justified. Instead, we take the risk of investing in others just as our Lord did. No prior experimentation can predict success.

A "theology" dictated by science will not lead in that direction. Only the "foolishness" of the cross—the gospel of God—will move us to commit to the church's mission, and to Christian communion as described in the New Testament.

All of this comes to bear on my friend Nathan, and the way this philosophy would guide our relationships with him. Could a theology dictated by the logic of science move us to act hopefully and redemptively in this "questionable cause"? Could a theology based on science teach us how to be the church of Jesus Christ toward Nathan?

Maximizing Enjoyment

Process philosophy and theology cannot lead us to the heart of the gospel and the soul of the church. It cannot tell us why we should invest the extreme time and energy Nathan's uncertain redemption will require. Let's explore.

"Enjoyment" is a primary factor in process philosophy. As an actual occasion (the smallest unit of process) achieves its momentary fulfillment, it subjectively "enjoys" its accomplishment. But when its process of emergence (concrescence) and enjoyment are complete, an actual occasion becomes a *datum* or object for a new concrescing actual entity—a new process—to take into account. Each actual occasion should strive to maximize its potential for enjoyment and novel value. What the occasion has achieved becomes the *datum* not only for succeeding actual occasions but also for God. It is potential for God's own ever-enriching subjective "enjoyment." God enjoys the world. God's overarching aim for the world is that it maximize its enjoyment and hence maximize God's own enjoyment. That which diminishes enjoyment should be avoided for the sake of the world and for God's sake.

Here is the rub between process thought and the gospel. The sacrifices Nathan's possible redemption would require would minimize—not maximize—the enjoyment and harmony of the congregation. There would be more congregational enjoyment if he were not around. I could visit more lonely people, help more struggling marriages, have more time for study, and preach better sermons.

There is no way to obey the gospel and at the same time maximize the enjoyment expectations of process philosophy. If calculating and maximizing the potential for enjoyment is what human life and God are about, then investing in Nathan—as required by being the church of Christ—is a foolish waste of good potential. The process vision of what God expects of the world makes absolutely no place for Nathan, and hence no place for the church composed of redeemed sinners.

Process philosophy cannot tell us why we should leave the ninety-nine sheep to search for the one lost sheep. What kind of value calculus is it that leaves ninety-nine for one?

The critique can move even further. The process God who strives for harmony and enjoyment would encourage Christians to look at one another that way. Harmony and enjoyment would be uppermost. "Process theology," Cobb and Griffin tell us, "sees God's fundamental aim to be the promotion of the creatures' own enjoyment."[6] We should treat one another with mutual and universal *enjoyment* in mind. Actions that lead most directly to universal enjoyment are good ones; actions that distract from universal enjoyment are bad ones. Nathan is left out of this model.

The meaning of sin also changes as we strive for enjoyment. The Bible teaches that sin is "missing the mark"—failing to love the Lord our God with all our hearts, and our neighbors as ourselves. Process philosophy and theology establish another "mark"—mutual, universal enjoyment. The most "holy" actions are ones that lead to the most happiness (enjoyment) for the greatest amount of creatures, as well as for God. So, process thought relies on a moral calculus to decide actions and set responsibility. Investing in Nathan, as the gospel of Jesus Christ requires, will fail the test. We are in the presence of two radically different estimates of the church and Christian discipleship.

For process thought, in order to make decisions that best advance universal enjoyment, an accurate *perspective* is required. After all, an action that seems to promote enjoyment—what appears to be loving—might turn out not to promote enjoyment on a grander scale. True to the sciences, careful observation should lead one to broader perspectives and hence to more accurate decisions about what would maximize enjoyment. Expanding our perspective on how to maximize enjoyment should help Christians make choices that justify how they expend their time and energy. Christians should still love their neighbors and pray for their enemies. But when making decisions about how best to invest our limited time and energies, we should weigh the cost against the benefit. If not, we might minimize the community's enjoyment. We can love everyone, but we should "buy stock" in persons most likely to yield the greatest measure of enjoyment.

Utilitarian Love

At their core, process philosophy and theology are fundamentally *utilitarian* in character (the greatest measure of good or value for the greatest number of persons; also called *consequentialism*). If we adopt the process God's way of acting, we will try to appropriate God's perspective for our own. We will make choices that promise the greatest measure of universal harmony and enjoyment. We have access to calculated probabilities as our guide. This helps us choose the course of action that promises to bear much fruit, eliminate conflict, and promote the greatest measure of harmony in the world.[7]

Process theology's scientific (calculating) utilitarianism is most often expressed in terms of love. But it is a love that would finally make no place for Nathan. Whitehead said, "The greater part of morality hinges on the determination of relevance [for] the future."[8] Love must promote future universal well-being (enjoyment). Anything that does not promise this is unloving.[9] This requires taking into account as many factors as possible. Specific enjoyment must conform to universal enjoyment.

David Griffin counters that Whitehead is not a "strict utilitarian." Only "the greater part" of morality is to be decided on a cost-benefit analysis. This is a weak objection; it is not at all clear which dimensions of morality Whitehead withholds from utilitarian calculation.

If Whitehead is correct, then the rules of utilitarianism (consequentialism) must be applied to how the church carries out its mission, and to forming individual discipleship. Godly actions should pursue the greater good, even if Nathan, or a minority group, must suffer as a result. Some process representatives have unsuccessfully tried to avoid this conclusion. Charles Hartshorne talked about "contributionism," which refers to the way every event contributes to a common future.[10]

But by this logic, energy expended on Nathan's behalf remains ill-advised. He is not likely to contribute to a better future, nor am I likely to contribute well when I attend to his needs. Whitehead developed a theory of virtue and claimed that pure utilitarianism is untenable. Nevertheless, for him virtue is still determined by an analysis of the greatest measure of possible and probable enjoyment and value.[11] Clearly, committing the energies needed to help Nathan will not pass the test of probability.

So in the end, despite occasional objections to my charge, a utilitarian, calculating estimate of whether we should invest in lost causes remains. In spite of all the rhetoric about humility, relationship, and love, the ultimate arbiter remains the calculating rational self; what will maximize individual and universal enjoyment?

The Foolishness of the Gospel

All this is fundamentally at odds with the foolishness of the cross, the church as Christ's agent of redemption in the world, and Christian discipleship that shoulders lost causes like Nathan.

There are more academic-like reasons for saying process philosophy and apostolic Christian faith are incompatible. But it is process philosophy's primary motif—maximizing enjoyment for the world and God—that prompts my strongest objection. If process philosophy remains consistent with itself, it cannot comply with the gospel of Jesus Christ. Nathan and others like him demonstrate the gulf that exists between the utilitarian logic of process philosophy and the kingdom of God as presented in the New Testament.

In Jesus' ministry—his proclamation that, in him, the Kingdom was being inaugurated—he regularly gave himself to the lost causes of Israel—beggars, lepers, prostitutes, prodigal sons, and tax collectors. Process philosophy could not have supported Jesus without betraying itself.

The New Testament calls for a church, and a quality of discipleship, that rejects calculated cost-benefit analysis. Instead, it calls us to a sacrificial love that welcomes Nathan even though the likelihood of success is low. The gospel moves us to welcome Nathan as a returning prodigal, even if he is on his seventy-seventh trip back home (Matt. 18:21-35). Only the gospel of Jesus Christ, not process philosophy, makes a place for Nathan, the one lost sheep (Luke 15:3-7), or the one lost coin (Luke 15:8-10). He is the traveler beaten and left to die (Luke 10:25-37), and the "least of these" with whom Jesus identified (Matt. 25:40).

The logic of process theology with its undergirding utilitarian foundation cannot be made to comply with the foolish investments these pivotal gospel stories relay. When process theologians claim otherwise, they betray fundamental process commitments. Whitehead famously called God a "fellow-sufferer who understands."[12] But all Whitehead's God could understand about Nathan is that he is probably a hopeless case that should warn us to cut and run.

Conclusion

As I sat talking to Nathan, thinking about all the more pressing things I needed to do, it dawned on me that foolishness, not enjoyment, is at the heart of the gospel. We are called to act out of hope for Nathan, not because of what Nathan promises, but because of what Christ the Redeemer promises. That, not process philosophy, is the proper model for the church and Christian discipleship. Dropping everything to help Nathan is *good,* even if it doesn't produce success in the long run. So far as I know, it never did.

The New Testament intentionally separates commitment to "the least of these" from the logic of maximized success. A theology fundamentally indexed to scientific models—as is process theology—can never properly serve the gospel of Jesus Christ. It can never provide an adequate model for the church, and it can never form comprehending disciples of Jesus.

A predictable cause-and-effect model can never give birth to what Christian hope is all about. Hope for persons like Nathan—for all of us—is grounded in the resurrection of the crucified Jesus—when hope burst forth and broke the chains of hopelessness.

None of this dismisses the very practical challenges Christian congregations confront. There are bills to pay. Lawns must be mowed and sidewalks shoveled. The infirm must be visited, and families in crisis counseled. But the economics of productivity must not become the church's self-understanding or determine what to do with the Nathans.

Let us recall that in the Garden of Gethsemane Jesus overcame the temptation toward enjoyment. He prayed, "Not my will but yours be done" (Luke 22:42). When the Nathans appear at our doors, their faces contorted by pain and addiction, the Gethsemane struggle repeats for the church. "My way" is all about the economics of managing time, calculating the greatest return of enjoyment and harmony. The alternative that Jesus embraces, the way of his Father, is absurd and uncomfortable and unscientific. The church stands frequently at this very crossroads, between settling for the future we find possible or living toward a future that appears both foolish and impossible.

Process theism, I suggest, turns us toward the possible, toward the future we can anticipate and the causes and projects that make sense.

This is a good way to run a business, a good way to balance budgets, and a good way to win a battle. But Christian theology must do something profoundly different. It must offer hope for Nathan and attend to him as if he were Christ himself.

The future of the church is not the future we can predict, based on what we observe. An impossible future calls the church to be precisely what it cannot anticipate being: to lay down our scientific tools and hope in a beautiful and irrational future Jesus calls the kingdom of God.

Chapter 8 Outline

Introduction

What Happens to Evil?

What Happens to Sin, Grace, and Salvation?

    Sin

    Grace

    Salvation

Conclusion

8
What Becomes of Evil, Sin, Grace, and Salvation?
John W. Wright

Introduction

The news spread quickly through the small farming town where I ministered. A wife had escaped a horribly abusive husband. A year later she returned from a Bible college to sell her property. Her former husband showed up at the Saturday auction, pulled a gun, and killed his former wife (the sister of a member of my congregation). The man then turned the gun on himself.

That evening I met with my parishioner—brother of the murdered woman. It was Holy Saturday. We tried our best to pray and understand the horrible events of the day. The enormity of evil and sin settled over us. The next morning we were to celebrate the Feast of the Resurrection. Grief and confusion plagued me as I watched my parishioner walk into the sanctuary the next morning.

Evil and sin can confound the wisest of Christians. Process theologians are no less troubled. But they frequently claim they can make evil and sin more understandable than can classical theology. Like Job's *accusers* who seemed to have it all figured out, process theology relies upon a philosophical system to explain evil and sin. They claim to be able to isolate the problem and offer solutions. In the process, they explain the meaning of sin, grace, and salvation.

However, in the end, like Job's accusers who have complete rational explanations for Job's problems, process theology empties God, evil, sin, grace, and salvation of their transcendence and mystery. Instead of the holy and loving God of the Bible surprising us with grace, according to process theology humans help God achieve the world's and God's potential (salvation). Unpacking the difference between these two visions takes us to the heart of how differently process theology and historic Christianity understand evil, sin, grace, and salvation.

What Happens to Evil?

Answering the question requires us to first ask, "What does process theology mean by 'good'?" Process theologians often talk about what is good. But instead of "good" referring primarily to God's holiness and love, process theologians have in mind the beneficial results of what the world and God achieve. It refers to self-determination, acting to enrich value, and achieving novel value in the world. All of these come together in the idea of creativity. God promotes creativity; that is good. The world fulfills creativity; that is good. The world enriches itself and God by fulfilling its potential; that is good. Process theology grounds the good in the world, not in God. Further, creativity requires self-determination—what process thought calls freedom.

Next, for process theology good is not primarily of religious importance. It doesn't primarily have to do with God's goodness. Nor is good primarily associated with ethics. Instead, good is primarily a matter of *aesthetics*—the beautiful, lovely, and harmonious. The good is whatever adds to creativity, novelty, and beauty in the world. Understanding how God and the world work together to promote these things provides the key for understanding the process meaning of evil.

God interacts with the world to generate the best possible world. God then appropriates (feels) the world's achievements, incorporates them into his own consequent (temporal, concrete) nature, and thereby enriches (increases) his own life. It isn't much of a stretch to say that for process thought the value-enriched world then helps to create God anew. Each new phase in the God/world process provides the basis for a new future world and an expanded God. God leads by offering initial goals; the world follows well or poorly; and God subsequently increases by taking into himself (prehending) the world's achievements. On and on it goes.

We might say that process thought conceives of the world's development like a game of checkers. The first person (God) moves. That changes the board (history), and the thoughts of the other player (the world). The other player moves, and affects the board and the first player as well. The illustration falls short of process philosophy because checkers is played on a board where creativity is limited. By contrast, the process vision of reality is unlimited.

Each new version of the world comes from the past. The world's achieved values form the basis for God's ever-enriching and changing consequent nature (think of "consequent" as meaning "subsequent").

God's *primordial* (initial) activity is to offer the world its initial (initiating) aims for achievement. (Here we are speaking of God's primordial nature in which all the ideal possibilities for the world are lodged.) These aims constitute a hierarchy of values (some fulfilled aims would be richer in quality than others). From this hierarchy God offers what is best for each new actual occasion. The occasion—the smallest drop of reality and experience—must decide to accept or reject what God offers. Obviously, actual occasions must possess a measure of self-determination. Each one must decide what is best by selecting from the possibilities God offers.

Think of the eternal possibilities in God's primordial nature as a menu. The menu contains all the aims (divine recommendations) God might offer a newly emerging actual occasion. Now think of God as a waiter who brings the menu to the patron, but who cannot order from it. Think of a waiter who, after the meal, benefits from praise the patron heaps on the waiter.

Each new occasion possesses at least a measure of subjective freedom and self-determination. Humans will have more self-determination than a dolphin, and hence a greater capacity for creativity and value. Absent freedom there would be no creativity and hence no achieved value—what the process God values (and needs) most.

Now we are ready to understand what evil is. Is it the creation rebelling against its Creator? Is it a refusal to worship and obey the God who is Holy Love?

No. For process philosophy and theology, evil is the result of an actual occasion's failure to accept and achieve the optimum possibility God offered. Such failure can have either minimal or enormous consequences for others. Rejecting the premiere aim God has offered obstructs creativity. It minimizes the achievement of value. Emergence of ever-richer orders of value is always good. Outright rejection or even laziness that shortchanges the goal always results in evil.

Evil is the failure to achieve potential value; it also is the consequences of that failure. Evil can result at all levels of existence, including the subpersonal level. For example, even an amoeba can miss its potential. Evil becomes more noticeable and influential the more complex the occasion—especially in societies of occasions such as humans.

One final phase in the God/world relationship should be noted. As actual occasions reach their completion (the end of their concrescence; see glossary) God does something with the value and novelty they have freely achieved. He appropriates that value (feels or prehends it). He takes it into his own life—into his consequent nature. God feels not only the good that has been achieved but also the failures. Process theologians make much of "the God who feels our sorrows."

Next, God creatively preserves and reorders all the achieved value into an ever-increasing, ever-enriching harmony. This enriches God's own being in the form of his concrete pole or consequent nature. God grows and becomes more than he was before. God's past consequent nature perishes, only to become potential for God's subsequent future, just as actual occasions perish and subsequently become data for subsequent actual occasions. This shows how creativity applies to God just as it applies to other parts of the world. Yes, this means that God's consequent nature actually changes and that its future is largely dependent upon the world.

God always does his best to pull together all the accomplishments of actual occasions (actual entities) into the best possible order.

The following will sound strange to traditional Christians, who don't normally think of evil as positive. The countless errant past and present decisions for self-determination that fell below God's aim for them will still form part of God's consequent nature. All the scars of distorted self-determination are present in God. But they don't just lie there. God works to raise past evils to new forms by healing them. The results become part of the potential God offers future emergent actual occasions. The important thing to notice is that evil remains *in* God. Past evil is never fully expunged from God's consequent nature.

Here we need to register that not one line in the Bible supports the notion that God necessarily absorbs evil into his own life.

Process theology claims its account of evil has two advantages over traditional Christian theology. *First,* process theology describes how evil happens even while God remains good. The process God doesn't create the world and doesn't reign over it. So he doesn't have to account for evil. God remains eternally good. In his primordial nature (eternal pole) God eternally values creativity and harmony and never fails to offer the best goals to emergent actual occasions. If actual occasions reject what God offers, God remains perfect. If the world rejects what God offers, don't blame God. The world, in its failures to be properly creative, gives rise to evil. God never coerces an actual occasion to accept the good purpose God offers. God has finite power, but even so, he exercises it flawlessly.

Process theologians say this explanation should encourage piety. There is no longer any reason to ask, "Why didn't God stop the murderer?" There is no longer any reason to blame God for child and spouse abuse. God could not have prevented the evil without forcing the perpetrator. Forcing someone to do what is good would fundamentally violate how God/world is structured. It would require overpowering the "sacred" subjectivity of the offender. It would violate the character of relationship. And it would overturn how God/world works. Now, pious folk can pursue the good and oppose evil without raising the same religiously troubling questions about the process God, which they often raise about the sovereign God of traditional Christianity.

Furthermore, God feels evil. Even though the process God cannot stop evil from happening, he is a fellow sufferer. He feels the world's sorrow and even takes them into his own life. The consequent nature of God is full of pity.

With the preceding explanation in place, let's critique it from the perspective of historic Christian doctrine. The process explanation is deeply flawed when judged by traditional Christian faith.

First, we should recognize the moral dangers that follow from assigning creativity the prominence it receives in process thought. The logic of maximizing creativity leads to the very thing process theologians say they oppose. Remember, for process thought, maximizing creativity is job number one. It's creativity first and foremost. Anything that gets in the way of creativity is evil. Think of the implications. A colonial power can justify exploiting a weaker country in the interest of maximizing its own creativity. A powerful industry can exploit the resources of an underdeveloped country to maximize profits. The small nation has limited capacity for creativity. The rich nation has far more. Is not the best way to maximize creativity clear? Failure to dominate the weaker country will be evil by process standards. A superior culture can (must) produce more value than a technologically backward culture. How to maximize value in the inferior culture seems clear.

Creativity and novelty can contribute to and participate in the good. But creativity, when given the importance process assigns, can also pervert what is good and lead to an end we recognize as evil.

Second, process thought becomes trapped in a counterproductive notion of freedom—freedom viewed as self-determination (remember the subjective, sealed freedom of the emergent actual occasion uncontrolled by what is outside its subjectivity). The greatest evil process theology can imagine is external and forced limitation upon self-determination. Everything that is ethically commendable and defensible includes self-determination.

No doubt, self-determination can be a good. However, it is not an unqualified good. Unless self-determination is guided by some higher good it becomes personally and socially destructive. History is stocked with examples. Judas is one illustration. Self-determination must be secondary to virtue.

Third, according to the process explanation, evil is primarily a matter of aesthetics, a failure to achieve beauty, value, and harmony. By contrast, in traditional Christian faith, evil is primarily a religious problem. It results from the creature's refusal to worship God as God. But for process theology, evil is primarily an offense against creativity, beauty, and harmony, not against God.

There is no way to reconcile these two perceptions of evil. One is primarily an offense against the world and its possibilities. The other is an offense against the holy and loving Creator. One is interested in harmony, the other in obedient worship. Process theology cannot begin to embrace the meaning of worship in the great Christian tradition: the creature recognizing that he or she is a creature and that God alone is Creator. Worship is a comprehensive act of submitting to and ordering oneself in compliance with the Creator and Redeemer.

Fourth, the process solution to the problem of evil is quite flawed. God's cosuffering with us doesn't solve a thing. Process theologians have only sentimentalized God.

Let's go back to that Easter-eve discussion with my parishioner. I could have explained to him God's total innocence in the situation. God was doing the best he could. I could have assured my brother in Christ God was suffering with him. But, had I done so, I would have offered no hope—certainly not the hope of the resurrection. Such "comfort" would have reeked of impotence.

The Christian hope for the end of evil doesn't reside in a God who is sympathetically taking evil into himself. It certainly does not lie in assurance that God has heard our grief and somehow in the future will work it into something good. Instead, it resides in the resurrection of the Christ who has conquered death, hell, sin, and the grave on our behalf, who will return to consummate his Kingdom, and who will raise and transform our mortal bodies. He *will* consummate new creation.

The violent former husband could kill his former wife. But the Heavenly Father could raise her to eternal life through Jesus Christ and give her conscious, eternal blessedness. Let it be clear. The process God knows absolutely nothing of this.

What Happens to Sin, Grace, and Salvation?

What process theology teaches regarding sin, grace, and salvation is closely related to what it teaches about evil. *Sin* is personal evil, or evil an individual generates. Its effects are sweeping. *Grace* describes the ideal possibilities God offers. *Salvation* refers to God incorporating into his consequent nature the outcomes of the aims he offers the world.

Sin

Process theology's understanding of sin is distinctly relational and hence relative. Sin is not a violation of the revealed will of a holy God. It does not refer to behavior that contradicts the character of God. Instead, sin refers to how persons interact in relationship with each other, including God who is a particular kind of person. That relationship is anchored in the relationship between self-determination and the high aims God offers.

God seeks to maximize creativity and novelty in the world, while preserving "freedom." Freedom is intensely organic or interactive. If a person refuses God's aim, his or her refusal diminishes what others can accomplish—including God. If we diminish another person's potential for creativity and value, we sin. Sin is primarily a violation against another person's potential—including God. It is a matter of infringing against creativity and value in the world. For process thought, the world is the ultimate category—a single reality that includes God, humans, and everything else. So, sin is this-worldly. The world—the ultimate and final scene of creativity and value—is sinned against.

The difference between traditional Christian doctrine and process theology in how they understand sin can hardly be overstated. For apostolic Christian faith, sin is first of all disobedience against God. It is refusal to worship him as God and to live in loving compliance with his will. Fundamentally, sin claims for the creation what belongs to God alone. That is, sin treats the world as ultimate and tries to make God just another part of it. As with process theology, sin is indeed sin against other persons. But for historic faith, that is a secondary result of the primary offense—refusing to let God be God in the world.

Grace

Here we meet a strange twist in the difference between classical Christian faith and process theology—one that puts them light-years apart.

At first the difference is not apparent. For process theology, grace is understood as God giving an ideal initial aim to each actual occasion. God takes the first step, so to speak. Grace is absolutely necessary for an actual occasion, or society of actual occasions such as a person, to become anything concrete. This is true for all actual occasions. So we can see that grace in this respect is universal. To this point there is a similarity between process theology and traditional Christian doctrine. But then the disjunction between the two erupts.

Not only is the world dependent upon God, for process thought God is dependent upon the world. If God makes the world's concreteness possible, no less does the world make God's concreteness possible. God's consequent nature is totally dependent upon the achieved value the world provides.

Here is the amazing twist. Not only does God give grace to the world by providing the ground for its concrete achievements, but the world *gives grace* to God by providing the basis for God's concreteness. Otherwise, God would be mere possibility (primordial nature). Both God and the world can sing, "Amazing grace, how sweet the sound . . ."

Just as the world grows in grace, so does God. Growth in grace is what the God/world is all about! How marvelous! God reaches his fulfillment through grace. But can anyone find a shred of support in the Scriptures and apostolic Christian faith for such a notion?

Process theologians never tire of telling how process thought amplifies Christian doctrine. One is justified in wondering how this can be true when process theology departs so radically from one of the most fundamental Christian doctrines.

Salvation

For process theology, salvation involves a person accepting God's aim for his or her maximum creativity. But salvation doesn't end there. God acts in many ways to draw persons into the "fullness of the kingdom of God." God also redeems by preserving (remembering) all the moment-by-moment values each person achieves. Nothing of value is lost. The process is unending.

But notice, just as God saves the world, the world saves God. As God saves the person, the person saves God. There is simply no way of getting around it; God needs to be saved just as does the world. God's remembrance (redemption) of the world is God's own salvation—the formation of God's consequent and completing nature. Just as God eternally brings forth the world's potential in history, even so the world brings forth God's potential in history. Just as God contributes to the world's eternal future, the world contributes to God's eternal future.

Again, the yawning chasm between this and apostolic Christian faith leaves one wondering about the legitimacy of calling process theology Christian.

Conclusion

Our brief tour of how process theology understands evil, sin, grace, and salvation has exposed significant differences between process theology and historic Christian doctrine. The differences are so great they can't be overcome unless one party is willing to conform to the other. Neither one appears to be willing to do that. A deliberate choice between the two must be made.

I choose the one that leads to Easter faith. That is the faith in which the church's hope is grounded, and the only faith worthy of commendation to grieving families and congregations

Chapter 9 Outline

Introduction

Eliminating Theological Options

First a Cosmology

A Comprehensively Ordered Whole

A "Consumerist" God

A God Who Competes with the World

What Becomes of Community?

No Radical Openness to the Future

Another "Gospel"?

9

What Becomes of Community, the Neighbor, and the Dispossessed?

Craig Keen

Introduction

I first made serious contact with process philosophy when I was a seminary student in 1973. I studied three of Alfred N. Whitehead's books that fall, including much of his *Process and Reality*. I had majored in biology my first two years of college and found Whitehead's scientific inclinations a delightful reminder of the way biologists and chemists look at the world. I had also majored in philosophy and was hungry for the vision his texts provided. I was so taken by process philosophy and the prospect of a process theology that I applied for admission to the Ph.D. program in Philosophy of Religion and Theology at Claremont Graduate University, the center of the world for process studies. I was admitted the fall of 1975 and enrolled immediately in an Advanced Seminar in Whitehead. It was taught by John B. Cobb Jr., the world's leading process theologian. It was *the* time to study process theology. Although over thirty years later it still has some impressive advocates and there are still young process theologians who may have an impressive future, process theology is no longer fashionable.[1] Yet in 1975 it was among the most promising American theological contenders.[2]

It did not take me long, however, to grow weary of process theology. While I was taking the course in Whitehead, I also took one in Martin Luther taught by Jane Dempsey Douglas, and one in the interpretation of human life with Wolfhart Pannenberg, visiting professor from the University of Munich. It is hard to imagine a theology more at odds with Whitehead than Luther's. I caught his passion for the cross of Jesus.

Pannenberg was the most knowledgeable and intelligent person I had ever met. Not only did his work draw upon the full range of subjects Whitehead engaged, but it was decidedly *theological*. Pannenberg's jabs at process theology, combined with Luther's vision of the God of grace clothed in the flesh of Jesus, slowly opened my eyes to Whitehead's paganism. I began to see process theology's failure to engage in any serious criticism of Whitehead's philosophy. Any supposed "Christian" theology that defines "the way, the truth, and the life" elsewhere than in the history of Jesus is not to be taken seriously. This holds doubly when *Jesus* is required to conform to some outside definition of "the way, the truth, and the life." Process theology makes this requirement.

The charge will be explained. I will provide eight reasons for my judgment. Each one builds upon its predecessor. We will see that process philosophy contradicts the gospel of Jesus Christ and the kind of community Jesus creates.

Process *philosophy* is an impressive intellectual exercise constructed creatively out of the intellectual goods of Western civilization. Process *theology*—process philosophy's child—makes a prior commitment to this system. *Process* philosophy comes first; process *theology* comes second.

The ideas of process philosophy and process theology are impressive. They are Whitehead's ideas, more often than not.[3] Whitehead was brilliant. He was one of the world's leading mathematicians and logicians. He was a competent historian of ideas. Whitehead drew from the philosophy of the ancient Greeks[4] and early modern Europeans.[5] He drew from evolution theory, relativity theory, and quantum mechanics; from sociology, psychology, biology, chemistry, and physics. He loved aesthetics—art, music, and poetry. Reared in the home of an Anglican priest, Whitehead appreciated religious sentiment and piety.[6] He was educated in the classics and had a romantic spirit. He looked at the world and wondered. He looked at his own inner life and probed. He knew elation and distress, love and despair. And he was determined that his philosophy not forget any of this.

Above all, Whitehead was a synthesizer. He had a rare gift for weaving a coherent system of ideas out of what at first seemed an irreconcilable heap of contrasts and contradictions. He aimed to take in everything that he could, and from as many sources as possible. He sought to speculate, but without forgetting the hard empirical facts that populate the universe and without forgetting the delicacy of experience. Whitehead aimed to be coherent, adequate to the facts, logical, and ready to revise. The result is most impressive, not unlike a majestic musical composition. However, not all music or philosophy glorifies God.

Let's examine eight features of process theology that will, together, answer, "What Becomes of Community, the Neighbor, and the Dispossessed?" Each feature will build upon its predecessor until we reach the conclusion.

Eliminating Theological Options

As a coherent and comprehensive system, process philosophy eliminates certain theological possibilities for theologians who identify with it. These include beliefs absolutely crucial to the Christian faith. Process philosophy is like the large and impressive country estate of an English lord, surrounded by an insurmountable wall. The estate seems roomy at first, but its wall stands tall to keep you locked in and others locked out. Process philosophy domesticates the world—and would domesticate Jesus. It may also be compared to the ninety-nine safe and one lost sheep. It claims to be open to all. As we shall see, in truth it is only open to the ninety-nine safe sheep—those who can be confined. It excludes from the fold the one lost sheep—the outcasts of the world—because the system will not accept them. What is *other* than the system will always be left outside. Only what *fits* "inside the philosophical wall" and "inside the fold" is good enough to include. This includes sinners and much of orthodox Christian faith. The philosophy of Whitehead is tolerant—even inclusive—but not to the point of permitting its own coherence, beauty, and advancement to be disrupted.

First a Cosmology

Process philosophy is first a cosmology (a comprehensive explanation of the origin and character of the universe, including humanity's place in it). What it says about "God" is pasted onto its picture of the universe as a totality.[7] God's significance is decided in advance by what "cosmos" means and requires. God's meaning and importance are secondary; they are decided by God's role in and service to the world (for example, God is needed to provide "aims" and "lures" for the world's potential). Because "God" is secondary to "cosmos," process theologians cannot affirm the traditional doctrine that God created the universe out of nothing (creation ex nihilo).

For instance, the traditional doctrine of creation makes the universe utterly dependent on *God's* good pleasure. It is only what *God* freely gives it to be. But process thought reverses the order. God is what the *universe* gives (permits) God to be. Only as the world achieves its potential can God achieve God's potential. God is an "accident" (by-product) of "creativity," to use Whitehead's technical language.[8] So, process thought most reveres the universe.[9] It is the universe *first* and God *second*. It is unthinkable for the God of this cosmology to judge the world.[10] Instead, the world finally judges and limits God.[11]

A Comprehensively Ordered Whole

Although at first a cosmology, process theology becomes a sweeping *abstract* vision of all places and times, all things and persons—past, present, and future. The vision is held in place intellectually within a comprehensively ordered whole. Thus process theology removes the theologian from the *concreteness* of lived life. It demands him or her to assume a position of detached, safe neutrality from which the ways of the universe and its most esteemed inhabitant (God) may be observed, analyzed, and coordinated. Theology is no longer first and last prayer to God and love for neighbor. It is no longer an act of adoring the Sovereign Redeemer and journeying with Jesus Christ into solidarity with the world's lost sheep. Process theology is much more interested in being *right* than being *righteous*, being whole than being holy, and laying hold of the fruit of its own labor and yours, than following the humiliated Jesus Christ to the cross.

A "Consumerist" God

The God of process thought is a "consumerist" God. God can never author the self-giving fellowship of the Holy Spirit we meet in the New Testament. As a mode of detached thinking, process theology places itself outside what it observes and synthesizes. It picks and chooses what is valuable from the goods it holds in its mental gaze. This is not accidental. Selectivity perfectly matches the process vision of the world as a whole. Its universe is populated by inherently "consumerist entities"[12] (emerging actual occasions) that pick and choose. How so? It sees the world as filled with autonomous individuals, with each achieving its "satisfaction"—its individual fulfillment. This happens in sealed privacy or isolation from other equally autonomous individuals. Each internally sealed individual picks and chooses from available options (both facts and possibilities) in order to reach a certain private "satisfaction" (completion). The objectionable is left behind.

What is perhaps most horrifying is that the process "God" is the most *consumerist* of all entities. God coaxes (lures) the things of the world to develop. God leads them to achieve the greatest possible intensity of feeling—

precisely because God will eat them when they're dead.[13] God "consumes" their achieved value and is enriched as a result. Finally, God is unreservedly out for private satisfaction. Whitehead's "fellow sufferer [God] who understands" is the beef eater who fattens cattle to devour them.

A God Who Competes with the World

Whitehead's God competes with the world. The universe is conceived in such a way that making space for other entities requires that God be diminished. That is the meaning of the process term "co-creativity." Everything struggles to bring together in new ways what remains of the dead (the past events or "occasions" that have finished their journey). God provides the focus (the goal) for each emerging entity (occasion) and coaxes or lures it to include as much of the past as possible. But it is the emerging entity that makes the final determination about what it will be. God can only make the hard sell. Unlike the God of the Bible, the process God determines the outcome of nothing. We are sovereign co-creators with God precisely because process theology can't conceive of God's power except as in competition with everything else. That it is the outgoing and loving freedom of God that gives us freedom—as opposed to our own sovereignty—is more than Whiteheadians can entertain. For them, freedom demands that God "back off" and leave the world and us in control.

What Becomes of Community?

It follows, then, that process theology concentrates on the individual in a way that makes true community impossible—especially the kind of community that exists between God and God's people, and in Christ's church. This may seem counterintuitive, since process theologians never stop talking about "relationships." However, as was noted above, "relationship" means that only *what was*—the completed past—contributes to my identity. In turn, my identity contributes to *what will be*—the future. There can be no immediate relationships (communion) between living entities. Isolated, I alone occupy the moment in which I am presently alive. The moment that I *now am* is a complete solitude, a lonely instant of self-determination into which no one else, not even God, can enter. God suggests and lures—then gets out of the way. I alone—utterly alone—decide.[14] God and the neighbor are outside. So, when Whitehead says that religion is what one does with one's "solitariness," he really means it.[15]

Especially sad is that in the process vision of the universe there is no beginning and no end. The world always has been and always will be in some form (recall that the world is necessary for God's "existence"). The only things that begin and end are the isolated moments (the actual occasions) that come to be and end in lonely privacy. The most "real" is "the solitary individual," the secluded instance of integrity, the true wholeness. When the individual moment in the ceaseless flow of creativity falls away (having achieved its satisfaction), it makes its contribution to new things that happen, including God's own growth. God increases by enjoying what was achieved. God preserves the past in this way, as a kind of undying collector of achieved value.

Such an immortal cosmos, extending infinitely into the past and the future, reduces each particular event to the mathematical equivalent of zero.[16] That is, though individual events are retained in God's memory, they are retained with diminishing importance as God's own experience expands. Of course, that implies that no human life—not even the life of Jesus—can have permanent significance. Even Jesus of Nazareth is surpassed by God's ever-richer life and experience.

No Radical Openness to the Future

Process thought is "hopeless" when judged by the gospel of Jesus Christ. It doesn't intend to be. In fact, it champions "hope." It talks up the future, possibility, and newness. Yet there is in process theology no *radical* openness to the future, no possibility not restricted by the past. The future is but the result of pressure from the past and present. That the future might be given anew by God's creative grace is unthinkable. "Miracles" as the divine inbreaking of what had been impossible do not and cannot occur. "Miracles" are at best the actualization of certain rare possibilities already native to the universe as it is. "New" events just recombine remnants of old events in relatively new ways, but only in ways the universe permits. No real "new creation" happens as the New Testament claims and expects (John 3:1-16; 2 Cor. 5:17; Rev. 21:1-5).

Another "Gospel"?

We come finally to the most telling failure of all: Process theology is *incompatible* with the gospel that redeems sinners and is good news to the poor. There is no place in the system for those who have nothing of merit to contribute to God. Recall that process thought values what can enrich God and the world—beauty, coherence, symmetry. Failures such as lost sheep distract from the process God's enrichment—wholeness. So a process theologian would have to strain to agree with Paul that "God chose what is low and despised in the world, things that are not, to reduce to nothing things that are" (1 Cor. 1:28). Paul is speaking in light of the resurrection of the *crucified* Jesus. Through the lowly and despised crucified Jesus, God gives to the world all that God is. Such language has no place in the process vision of a self-enriching God. Process theologians cannot speak of Jesus' resurrection as Paul does, except as resuscitation of a corpse[17] or as a kind of minimal value retained in the composite unity of other entities, such as God.[18] The despised and crucified Jesus couldn't offer much that was desirable (1 Cor. 1:18-25).

The New Testament hope of the resurrection of the dead is that God will gloriously transform what "is not"—"slumdogs" (1 Cor. 1:26-31). But process thought would require of us some contribution, some achievement. Hence, process philosophy cannot understand God's love as a gaping openness to poor sinners who are radically different from God and who have nothing of merit to contribute to resurrection. Nor can process thought explain how God comes humbly to us who have taken far more than we have given.

If "love" is but a code word for building "relationships" with those who are likely to contribute to my own satisfaction, my own enrichment, then the value of other persons collapses into a heap of investments and returns. I give only so long as I can get—and get more. A long tradition of romanticism has taught us to think of love as a self-centered relationship in which "you complete me" or "you make me happy" or "my life would be empty without you."

In the gospel, however, love turns out to be something very different from a guarded, self-centered investment. God freely gives all that God is to those who have no riches to give in return, and to those of us who have taken more than we can give in return. "God proves his love for us in that while we still were sinners Christ died for us" (Rom. 5:8). What God has done, God expects us to do. "Just as I have loved you, you also should love one another" (John 13:34). "Let the same mind be in you that was in Christ Jesus, who . . . emptied himself . . . and became obedient to the point of death—even death on a cross" (Phil. 2:5-8).[19]

"The Father and I are one," the Gospel of John says (10:30). Where Jesus goes, the Father goes. Where the Father goes, Jesus goes. By the process standard of investment and return, God's love does what is impossible when Jesus—and his Father—travel the long road to Golgotha . . . and beyond. This is the story of God's entry into solidarity with the otherwise hopelessly lost of the world. It reaches its explosive end when Jesus is crucified along with men considered dregs of the world. Jesus' story is inseparable from theirs—from ours. "God was in Christ" on the cross with dregs! God descends with Christ into death, into solidarity with the most lost: "My God, my God, why have you forsaken me?" (Mark 15:34).

On Easter Sunday God's reply is, "I am here with you in the cold, dark hopelessness of death, with you and with this world's dregs." This is a newly climactic moment, one that quietly outdoes the first. It is not a reversal of Good Friday and Holy Saturday, but their glorification. The whole fullness of God is pleased to dwell where the world, where process philosophy expects that God cannot dwell. God comes to dwell with the outcast, the abandoned, the "God-forsaken." Such people by definition are excluded from the well-ordered whole that process philosophy conceives. They are blights on the orderly cosmology it describes and cherishes.

But "good news" for the blemishes, the blights, the dregs is what the gospel is all about. Even "God-forsakenness" (thinking oneself forsaken by God) cannot separate us from the love of God in Christ Jesus (cf. Rom. 8). In Christ, God is *for* the cosmic blight—all persons. The majestic process vision of God and the world has no place for such a God.

If "the poor" are those from whom life is being drained, then *the* "us" in the "God with us" of Good Friday and Easter Sunday signifies the poor in particular. God loves everybody, but always on the way to loving and reaching the poor. That is why the good shepherd leaves the ninety-nine in search of the one lost sheep. No consistent process theologian would engage in the extravagance of leaving the ninety-nine who "fit" so as to draw close to one lost sheep. He or she certainly would not commend a God who plummets into the darkness of death so that those whom the world despises will not be left to die alone.

Chapter 10 Outline

Introduction

The Familiar

The Strange

    God's Freedom

    God's Faithfulness

    Grace

Conclusion

10
What Becomes of God's Continuing Relationship to the World?
Al Truesdale

Introduction

An unsettling realization that we are in strange territory has seized most of us. It might happen in the middle of the night in a hotel room. We rise, half awake, take a few steps, stumble over a chair or bump into a wall that "shouldn't be there." It hits us. "This isn't home." Or, we may be driving in a strange city and turn onto a busy street. Momentarily everything seems normal. Suddenly we gulp. Both lanes of traffic are coming our way. "It's a one-way street!"

This resembles the response many Christian theologians have when they encounter process theology. Initially, much of the language seems familiar. They feel at home. After closer examination—perhaps after stumbling over statements about God—they realize they are in territory alien to apostolic Christianity. Two moods—the *familiar* and the *strange*—strike us when comparing process theology and classical Christian faith regarding God's relationship with the world. Let's examine the two.

The Familiar

Initially we may be attracted by process theology's statements regarding God's relation to the world. Similarities between biblical language and process theology abound. Far from God standing aloof from the world or being threatened by active engagement in it, according to the Bible and process theology, God is intensely involved. His often stormy relationship with Israel proves it. God's active presence in Israel's history shows engaging in the messy affairs of life does not jeopardize God's existence.

Similarly, according to process thought, God plans the best for all creation, makes his good will known, and actively urges the creation to fulfill its divinely offered potential. Though God's aims for the world are rich and comprehensive, he respects the varying levels of freedom the creation exhibits. The process God doesn't run roughshod over others to achieve his purposes.[1]

The process God comprehensively aims for increasing harmony in the creation. In love and wisdom, God works to redeem the past, unwilling to let miscarriages of purpose have the last word.

Not only is this true of individuals, but God employs the power of his love to achieve social justice though many currents push against it. God patiently and creatively works to include in community those who have been excluded because of contingencies they could not control.

The world is a scene of real meaning for God and humankind. God takes events seriously. Efforts to advance the frontiers of moral responsibility, medical care, and aesthetics are scenes of real novel accomplishment. Human history isn't a stage where a meticulously prearranged script plays out. Novelty is God's will, not his competitor.[2] For example: A daughter who spends years caring for her Alzheimer-plagued father adds moral value to the world.

Novelty and innovation in nature can also be observed in the world's evolutionary process.

Furthermore, moral, intellectual, and aesthetic accomplishments make a real difference in God's life. He experiences ("enjoys"), preserves, and is enriched by them. Why not? All parties to a loving relationship are enriched by accomplishments and pained by failures. Futility and loss will not overcome our struggle for justice, or the majesty of music and art. Time and human forgetfulness will not squander what love achieves.[3]

God preserves the richness of each experience by synthesizing its values and preserving them in the immediacy of his own life.[4] There is more. "This is the basis upon which God yet again offers providential influences to the world, guiding it toward its own finite reflection of God's infinite and everlasting life."[5]

Far from being extraneous to God, achieved value and beauty actually contribute to his *being* as God. God's *enjoyment* of the world and how he processes that *enjoyment* constitute his *consequent* nature (more about this later).

In numerous ways, mutuality between God and the world in process theology is more in harmony with the biblical picture of God than is true of much popularized Christianity. Often, process thought makes more sense of biblical language about God laughing, sorrowing, rejoicing, and repenting than does some traditional language that pictures God as an unfeeling and unaffected sovereign safely perched above the messy aspects of life. Process theologians speak often of the God of creative-responsive love[6] who "enjoys our enjoyments and suffers with our sufferings."[7] God *feels* the world's discord as well as its beauty. How else are we to understand God incarnate "greatly disturbed in spirit and deeply moved" before Lazarus' tomb (John 11:33)?

Process thought is better equipped to appreciate the reciprocity and vulnerability involved in covenantal love than are theologies that say in order to preserve God's sovereignty, God must be void of vulnerability. For process theology and for the Bible, any love—including God's love—that actively invests itself in another necessarily shoulders the risk of rejection. Void of vulnerability, love becomes abstract and superficial.

Vulnerable love—what other language is fitting for the Christ who emptied himself of divine privileges (stowed the "omnis" [omniscience, omnipresence, etc.]), assumed the life of a servant, and became obedient unto death (Phil. 2:5-11).

For Marjorie Hewitt Suchocki, the controlling theme of process theology is to call all Christians to live in anticipation of the reign of God, and a new future in history.[8]

The Strange

On closer examination, one discovers fundamental incompatibilities between process theology and apostolic Christian faith. We bump into things that shouldn't be there.

The fundamental incompatibility resides in *mutually exclusive* doctrines of God. In spite of what process theology claims, two different "Gods"—process and biblical-apostolic—are under consideration. The two cannot be reconciled. The differences bear directly on God's relationship with the world.

God's Freedom

God's freedom, as process theology understands it, is not what classical Christian doctrine teaches.

A. For process philosophy, "creativity" comes first. God comes later. Creativity is the most basic concept or category on which process philosophy builds. It is the primary and ultimate *principle* that makes concrete things possible. Novelty (the new) happens when the principle of creativity is applied to each situation.[9]

Don't think of creativity as "God" or as some concrete thing. It is a fundamental, constructive *principle* that gives rise to, and is embodied in, concrete things.[10] As "creativity" brings things into existence, creativity becomes *actual* (en-acted).

Think of creativity as *potential* for becoming something concrete. Think of it as becoming actively particular in something "concrete."[11] Time, for example, precedes and "embodies" a watch and calendar, not vice versa.

In the Bible, God comes first. He is the sole source of creativity. It has no meaning prior to him. All other forms of creativity are indebted to God the Creator. But for process philosophy, creativity transcends and precedes God.[12] Creativity makes God possible. God is the first instance of creativity. God and the world "embody" and "actualize" creativity. Clearly God is dependent upon a principle of reality that precedes him.[13]

The Bible and apostolic Christianity know of absolutely nothing that precedes or transcends God. "Has not my hand made all these things, and so they came into being?" (Isa. 66:2, NIV). God has no equal or superior (Isa. 40:25-31; 44:6-8). By biblical standards, process philosophy is idolatrous. It assigns primacy to something other than Yahweh. God's freedom has been fenced in by a superior predecessor.

Astonishingly, process theologians believe the process God and the God of the Bible can be reconciled. Equally astonishing is how they seem to ignore the theological implications of making creativity primary and God secondary.

B. Process philosophy distinguishes between God's *primordial* and *consequent* natures. God is *dipolar*. They refer to God's two distinctly different dimensions and functions.

The first "pole" or dimension is God's *primordial* nature or *eternal pole*. It contains the infinitely rich and harmonious array of God's aims for the world.[14] God's primordial nature is eternal (not temporal), unchanging, and abstract (not concrete). It comprehensively envisions the aims or goals (pure possibilities) God can offer to each concrete occasion of experience.[15]

If embraced, God's ideal aims become actual or concrete. An embraced *ideal aim* becomes an entity's *subjective aim*.

God's second pole is God's *consequent nature* or *physical pole*. As abstract and potential, God in his *primordial* nature is incomplete. God becomes complete as he takes into himself the world's achieved values, and its failures and heartaches. God "feels" the world's successes and failures. God creatively transforms what he "feels" or "prehends" (see glossary). The received "feelings" and their transformation constitute God's *consequent* nature. God is radically dependent upon the world.

Whereas God's *primordial* nature is eternal and unchanging, God's consequent nature is temporal and changing—increasing and enriching. The process of "becoming" applies to God.

For God to be complete there must be a world from which to derive his *consequent* nature. Only God as primordial and consequent deserves the name "God."[16] Process theologians sometimes speak of God's *primordial* nature as creative love, and of his *consequent* nature as responding love. As responding, God receives, preserves, and transforms in his own life the value the world achieves. "God as *fully actual* is responsive to and receptive of the worldly actualization."[17]

In turn, what the world achieves, or fails to achieve, affects God's primordial nature. God reconfigures the initial aims he will offer a world in process.

How unlike the God of the Bible! God the Creator is complete in himself before the world ever exists. The world is radically dependent upon God. Yahweh is the "Holy One" who "stretches out the heavens like a canopy, and spreads them out like a tent to live in" (Isa. 43:15; 40:22, NIV).

C. Let's contrast freedom as it relates to the process God and to the God of the Bible.

For process theology the world eternally and necessarily constrains God's freedom. It largely sets the boundaries of what God can do and become.

Unlike the God of the Bible, the process God actually *includes* the world in himself as constituting an essential "God" dimension.[18] God and the world form a continuum that "creativity" makes possible; they are mutually dependent. God and the world are co-eternal. Never was there a time when God "was" without a world of some kind.

When process theologians speak of the attractiveness of God's intense relationship with the world, they need to add that God has no choice in the matter.

By contrast, Yahweh is the *singular* source or cause of himself. The God of the Bible freely chooses to create the world and freely chooses to make covenant with us. Otherwise, John 1:1-18 and 3:16 are meaningless.

Though the process God can propose comprehensively, his "freedom" is indexed to what the world will or will not permit. The future is open only to the extent the world permits.

How unlike the triune God, who not only proposes and promises, but who has power to fulfill all his promises in Jesus Christ, even if it means "disarm[ing] principalities and powers," triumphing over them by the cross (Col. 2:15, NKJV).

The process God can never be truly free *for the world* because he is never *free from the world.*

The triune God on the other hand is free and complete *in* his own life. As the world's sole Creator and Sustainer, God is free *from* the world and hence free to be *for* the world. The twentieth-century Swiss theologian Karl Barth said, "[God] would be no less and no different even if all [created beings] did not exist or existed differently."[19] Process theology cannot say this.

The God of the Bible is also free *for the future.* The Old and New Testaments describe God as performing deeds the past could neither predict nor constrain. Both testaments declare the future is God's to create anew according to his sovereign will. To the Babylonian exiles Yahweh announced: "See, I am doing a new thing! Now it springs up" (Isa. 43:19, NIV). Those who are in Christ Jesus are "new creation[s]" (2 Cor. 5:17). The New Testament closes with the promise of "a new heaven and a new earth" (Rev. 21:1). Though historical circumstances are never ignored, no suggestion that God's freedom will be constrained by the past and settled ever surfaces. God is Lord of the world, not its client.

The incarnation of God in Jesus of Nazareth is the ultimate *new thing* God does. Did God first seek permission from what the world's past, or even Israel's past, would permit? No doubt the New Testament looks back to a long and continuous history of God's redemptive activity as seen in Israel's history and in broader world events. It sees Christ as fulfilling all God's promises (Luke 1:46-55, 67-79; 2 Cor. 1:18-22). But it does not present Christ as the natural development and climax of the past. The past did not have within it provisions for a crucified and risen Messiah. Instead, Jesus "is in one sense the catalyst who brings the grand story to its climax; in another sense he is the one who steps in and stops the downward spiral of these previous stories. A developmental model is insufficient when one is talking about interruption, correction, redirection, and indeed subversion of older stories."[20]

Can process theology speak this language? Not according to process theologian William Stegall. "There are limits on Divine power, as God has to work with what is given and is unable to exclusively determine the outcome at any given moment."[21]

Claiming these differences can be reconciled under the process umbrella requires too much of one's willingness to believe. Process philosophy is a wholly inappropriate and clumsy instrument for voicing the free God who surprisingly and definitively acts in the crucified and risen Christ to introduce the life-giving power of the end time (the eschaton) into history.

God's Faithfulness

Both process theology and the Bible make much of God's faithfulness (*hesed*), or constancy.[22] For process thought, God *never fails* to offer the best initial aims for each budding instance of existence, to lure it toward its potential, and to preserve its achieved value. At first this language seems familiar and reassuring. But upon closer examination, we learn that process language and the language of the Bible mean two different things when speaking of God's faithfulness.

For process theology, faithfulness is referenced *not* primarily to God's character as the Bible claims, but to the world. It isn't God's holy love that fixes his faithfulness, but his necessary dependence on the world. God doesn't *choose* to be faithful; it is metaphysically *required* of him.

Normally that isn't what faithfulness means. Faithfulness has a *volitional* quality such as when one chooses to be faithful to a friend or spouse. At first, when listening to process theologians, their language about God's faithfulness sounds volitional. But as it turns out, the process God has no choice in the matter. God always has and always will need a world in some form to achieve his own concrete life. So God's faithfulness must be redefined to include *inescapable mutual* dependence.

This doesn't apply to God's *primordial* nature (eternal pole).[23] But as we have seen, to speak only of God's primordial nature isn't to speak completely of God anyway. As noted earlier, for God to be complete, his consequent (physical) nature must be added. God as *fully actual* responds to and receives the world's actualization.[24] Only the concrete whole deserves the name "God."[25] Only abstractly does God transcend the world. Concretely, God is necessarily tethered to it.

The Old Testament celebrates God's faithfulness to the creation and to Israel. Two Hebrew words are prominently used for this purpose. The first is *hesed*, a word that has no exact English equivalent. It can mean God's lovingkindness or goodness extended to others. God "abound[s] in love [*hesed*] and faithfulness" (Exod. 34:6, NIV). He manifests constancy in dealing with his people. *Hesed* also means steadfast love, faithfulness, or loyal love. It binds two parties in a covenant relationship. So, *hesed* can include one person's faithfulness to another, Israel's faithfulness before God, and God's faithfulness to Israel and the creation. The second term is *emoonaw* (em-oo-naw). It means stability, steadfastness, faithful, and faithfulness. The word can refer to Israel's faithfulness before God. But most often it refers to God's faithfulness to others. "I will sing of your steadfast love [*hesed*], O LORD, forever; with my mouth I will proclaim your faithfulness [*emoonaw*] to all generations" (Ps. 89:1). Even in times of lamentation Israel could say, "The steadfast love of the LORD never ceases, his mercies never come to an end; they are new every morning; great is your faithfulness" (Lam. 3:22-23).

We can search the Bible's testimony to God's faithfulness from Genesis through Revelation and not find a hint that the world or Israel or the church is the ground, tether, or cause for God's faithfulness.

What is the primary reason for God's steadfast faithfulness? The answer reveals an unbridgeable gulf between process philosophy and the Bible. It confirms that in spite of all the familiar language, we are met by two different Gods.

The Scriptures testify that God's faithfulness is first of all *faithfulness to himself*, and only secondarily and freely faithfulness to the world. God's faithfulness rests totally upon his character—his person. He is unfailingly faithful to himself. "I am [Yahweh]; I act with steadfast love, justice, and righteousness in the earth, for in these things I delight" (Jer. 9:23-24). The psalmist declares God's "faithfulness surrounds" him (Ps. 89:8).

Because of this, from Genesis to Revelation the Bible declares God's faithfulness to his creation, to Israel, and to the church. The heavens praise God's wonders and the congregation of the saints his faithfulness (Ps. 89:5). Why else would Mary sing out, "My soul magnifies the Lord, and my spirit *rejoices in God my Savior*" (Luke 1:46-47, emphasis added)? For what other reason would Paul tell the Corinthian Christians that in Christ all of God's promises have been fulfilled (2 Cor. 1:20)?

The God who makes these promises is faithful to himself; hence he will be faithful to us. The faithfulness of Yahweh is simply not the faithfulness process theologians ascribe to the process God. The process God can be trusted because of the world. Yahweh can be trusted because of who he is. The thrice holy God whose glory fills all the earth (Isa. 6:1-5; Eph. 1:3-14) prompts our unqualified worship. The process God prompts our admiration.

Grace

Of all the Christian doctrines that seem most at home in process theology, grace is a principal candidate. Marjorie Hewitt Suchocki thinks so.

The boundless grace of God who is *"for us"* "bends to our condition, fitting divine harmony to the human situation."[26] God comprehensively offers rich possibilities for actualization to every instance of experience. He cherishes, preserves, and transforms all achieved value so that nothing is ever lost. Rather than acting as a coercive tyrant, God persuades and lures the world toward its potential.

The candidacy seems strong. But it fails. Again we encounter process theology's use of Christian language without submitting to governance by primary Christian doctrine. Grace is God's *free turning* toward us—toward the world—as Creator and Redeemer. It is radically unconditioned by any prior claims and is completely undeserved by its recipients. Grace comes in the radical absence of what has already been accomplished.

"Grace," Karl Barth explains, "cannot be called forth or constrained by any claim or merit, by any existing or future condition, on the part of the creature."[27] Grace unconditionally precedes the creature.[28] As soon as we introduce prior claims, foundations, or merit, grace becomes something else; it becomes *negotiation* no matter what we call it.

Therein resides process theology's erroneous appropriation of the Christian language of grace. What the process God does for the world is already and eternally conditioned by what the world has already accomplished. God hopes to add to the *already*. There never was a time when God could, in the absence of prior claims, act freely and graciously toward the world.

Process theology establishes a context for *negotiation* between what already is and what might be. The former conditions the latter. Theologian Robert Jenson sees this clearly. For process thought, the world has a "significance in itself" not a dependent pure gift from God.[29]

Conclusion

I ask two questions. How much in process philosophy and theology can we justify overlooking in order to say Christian faith is at home there? How much must we hear before we follow the bishops at the first Council of Nicaea, who clearly delineated between what is and is not Christian?

Chapter 11 Outline

Introduction

Christian Hope: Certainty or Wishful Thinking?

God Woos, but Cannot Coerce

God's Continuous and Gradual Activity

Process Eschatology: A Theology of the Possible

A Future Without the Resurrection

The Future Hope in Process Eschatology

Conclusion

11

What Becomes of the Consummation of the Kingdom of God, and Christian Hope?

Brent Peterson, Ph.D.

Introduction

Can Christians know with certainty that Christ will return to consummate the inaugurated kingdom of God? Will there be a general resurrection of the dead and the judgment thereafter? Will the whole creation finally recognize that "Jesus Christ is Lord, to the glory of God the Father" (Phil. 2:11)? Yes! Both are confidently affirmed by the New Testament and the Nicene Creed. We don't know the details as to how all this will unfold. We do know Christ will return and that his kingdom shall have no end (Rev. 11:15). This hope is usually associated with eschatology, the Christian doctrine that attends to last things. *Eschatology* comes from the Greek word *eschatos* (*es-cha-tos*), which can mean farthest, last, latest (Matt. 12:45; Mark 12:6).

Eschatology involves much more than the future. It includes the present healing, hope, and salvation found in the gospel of Jesus Christ. Jesus is the "eschaton"—God's definitive word and deed. The author of Ephesians says that in Christ, God's "plan for the fullness of time" was revealed. God is now "to gather up all things in [Christ], things in heaven and things on earth." This is the God who accomplishes "all things according to the counsel of his will" (Eph. 1:10; see vv. 7-14). So, eschatology involves what has already happened and what is yet to happen. The New Testament has no doubt about this.

Process theology also affirms that God is already working to bring about the Kingdom. Let us call that the promise of process theology. But underneath the promise lies a devastating peril that undercuts the confidence found in the New Testament and the creeds. Process theology says God presently works for the "redemption" of the world. And it *hopes* the kingdom of God will be fulfilled. However, it lacks the confidence that characterizes the

New Testament and historical Christian faith. The process God is not one who with certainty accomplishes "all things according to his counsel and will" (Eph. 1:11). Instead, process theology offers a God and future of *the possible—a possible God and a possible future*. Eschatology and Christian hope are inseparable. What God is doing and will do defines and inspires Christian hope. There are big differences between hope as the New Testament presents it and hope as described by process theology. We will examine some of the main differences. *First,* we will affirm the character of Christian hope.

Christian Hope: Certainty or Wishful Thinking?

Is Christian hope just wishful thinking? Is it like saying, "I hope the Seahawks win?" Or, "I hope my children will always love me." No! That kind of hope lacks certainty. Can hope involve certainty and still be hope? Does confidence in Christ's return and his completing the Kingdom involve more than saying, "I hope the Seahawks win"?

Hebrews 11:1 contains an unusual combination of words that captures the uniqueness of Christian hope. "Now faith is the assurance of things hoped for, the conviction of things not seen." We also learn from the New Testament that Christian faith—full confidence in God—is a gift from God (Rom. 12:3; Eph. 2:8). It is a confidence born of God's faithfulness. Faith is not the same as wishful thinking. But it also differs from the certainty that two times two equals four contains. There is an already and a not yet in Christian faith and hope. But there is no lack of confidence.

Let's illustrate. Recently I successfully defended my doctoral dissertation. The long process that led to this point was rewarding and challenging. Friends and colleagues would ask, "Brent, how is the dissertation coming?" Usually my answer was, "I am closer to the end today than I was yesterday." Each day I celebrated what I had so far accomplished. And each day I longed for completion. Some days I did not want to write. But the hope that one day the work would be completed gave me strength to continue. Even though there were hard and difficult days, I never doubted eventual completion. But I must admit that my confidence did not contain absolute certainty. Some people begin dissertations and never finish. Maybe their energy wanes. Perhaps they become too ill to continue. The dream of receiving a Ph.D. fades and then dies.

Take another illustration. When I was in the second grade, a television program invited viewers to send in a wish. The show received the wishes and granted some of them. I wrote a letter telling how much I wanted an Atari video game system. My cousins had one, and I thought I should have one.

I faithfully watched and waited. Surely the telephone would ring. My wish would be granted. I *hoped!* But truthfully, I doubted it would happen.

Hope and faith that I would finish my dissertation, or win the Atari, were more similar to wishful thinking than to Christian faith and hope. After three months I ceased watching the television program. But I continued with my dissertation. In both instances the quality of my hope shaped how I lived in the present and toward the future.

Do these two illustrations describe the Christian hope that one day Christ will return and that God's kingdom will be consummated? Is Christian hope a mixture of hope and "may-be"? Or does Christian hope involve absolute confidence?

In the New Testament, Christian hope is a matter of absolute certainty. What the Sovereign God began, he will complete, as promised. Christian hope is anchored in and renewed by the resurrection of Jesus Christ. The Father did not abandon his Son to the grave. He will not abandon his Son and his kingdom work now. God accomplishes all things "according to his counsel and will." And the Father has sent the Holy Spirit as the down payment on the redemption of God's people, "to the praise of his glory" (Eph. 1:13-14).

The New Testament speaks of God's dominion as the equivalent of sovereignty (John 18:36; 1 Pet. 4:11; 5:11; Rev. 1:6). New Testament scholar Ben Witherington III says Jesus and Paul were one in their "assumption that God had a purpose, direction, and goal for human history. Furthermore, they also are in agreement that God had intervened in that history to bring about its appropriate conclusion. In other words, they shared an eschatological worldview."[1]

Second, we can begin to examine the difference between Christian hope and process theology. Process theology offers a God of "purpose," but not of "dominion." We will be justified in asking whether a God without dominion can meet the expectations of Christian hope and eschatology.

An additional question needs to be in play. Is the Kingdom's coming something God accomplishes, something humans do, or some of both? Our answer will have profound implications for Christian hope, and for our confidence about whether the Kingdom will come in its fullness as God has planned and promised. Ben Witherington says the "dominion" to which Jesus refers when standing before Pilate (John 18:36) "is not something that human beings can create or cause to happen by organizing or by political or military action; it is something that happens through divine intervention. One can be a servant of such power or activity, but a human being cannot be its master or mastermind."[2]

How does process theology answer these questions about Christian hope? With certainty or with wishful thinking?

God Woos, but Cannot Coerce

How does process theology regard God's power. It is highly critical of the dominant historic Christian understanding of God's power. God's sovereignty has been a settled Christian doctrine even though Christians have endlessly debated its particulars. Nevertheless, God is believed to control human affairs as it serves *God's* wisdom and purpose. God has been thought of as all-knowing (omniscient) and all-powerful (omnipotent).

Process theology completely rejects the element of control in God's power. God's power is not of the kind that makes it possible for God to fulfill God's will just because God wants to.

According to process theologians, God has the power to offer goals (ideal aims) in all situations. God cannot under any circumstances fulfill God's will through coercion of any kind. But if God's purpose is freely embraced, God exercises the power of love to lure or woo all entities to fulfill God's aim for them. It isn't that God, out of love, grants freedom and then refuses to override it. Rather, each entity, each actual occasion, has an independent subjective freedom that God cannot violate. Anything God purposes for the world is necessarily limited by the world's unassailable freedom.

Process theologian David Ray Griffin makes this clear when discussing evolution, evil, and eschatology. He says the three topics are interrelated. Exploring how the physical universe evolved shows the direction the earth might take in the end. It shows what God can and cannot do to affect the process. Evolution also helps explain what God can and cannot do about evil.

Griffin uses the following illustration to explain how God lures but does not coerce. When a person is thirsty, God offers the desire to drink water to quench thirst. God provides a way—the desire to drink—to satisfy a need. This is called *appetition*. We have an "appetite," an attraction to water. But while God provides the appetite, God does not force us to drink. We must freely act on the offer. If we drink, we experience a physical satisfaction of our God-given desire. This can lead to more enjoyments such as thinking about the blessing of water.[3] This shows how God's aims can begin as quite simple. If acted upon, they can lead to higher satisfactions. Finding God "trustworthy," we can advance to greater trust in God. Coercion is not involved.

Process theology teaches that all finite things have a measure of subjectivity, of freedom and self-determination. Of course, freedom is relative to the finite thing in question. But it is there nonetheless. Humans have freedom relative to their natures.[4] God doesn't just leave each person alone and isolated with his or her freedom. Instead, God presents aims (goals) for all persons and then lures them to achieve God's aims. God acts first.[5]

God eternally offers the best aims possible. An upward trend in the long evolutionary process is discernible. The world as a whole, by way of evolution, is bending toward ever richer forms. More humane social structures are emerging. True, the process is slow and long. That is because entrenched and obstructive habits are in place and must be eased out. God, being persuasive, coaxes humans—indeed the whole world—to achieve novel forms of value, community, beauty, and so on.[6]

The proviso is that God is necessarily limited in what God can achieve. Natural law imposes limitations upon God. So does human response to divine aims that can be freely accepted or rejected. Without exception, God can accomplish only what the world makes possible. God works creatively within that range.

God's Continuous and Gradual Activity

Though there is no guarantee that what God proposes will be fulfilled, according to process theology God never quits. God always invites and urges humans—all things—to fulfill their reasonable potential. The future builds upon what has been achieved in the past and upon what is possible. David Ray Griffin says God's activity is *continuous*—always and everywhere exerting influence in agreement with initial aims. Divine activity is also *gradualistic*. It does not encourage creatures to achieve possibilities too different from their past.[7] God patiently works to join the future with what has already been achieved.

Griffin has described established boundaries upon what God can do and upon what can be confidently expected. God is limited to what the world's natural processes permit, to what the world in its achievements and failures makes possible. There can be no abrupt divine inbreaking, no divine intrusion into the present. Griffin explains that according to a naturalistic explanation of God's activity, "God cannot unilaterally bring about a state of justice, peace, and happiness."[8] Possibilities for the future are closely indexed to what has already been achieved.[9]

Who determines what is possible? Clearly, the process God is eternally constrained by what humans (and others) make possible. Process theology embraces the possible. But it rejects any future clearly discontinuous with the past. This would mean that the "new" that happened in the incarnation of God in Jesus of Nazareth, and Jesus' resurrection, cannot and does not happen. Both of these violate "continuity" with the "evolutionary" past. Christian doctrines must be restated in agreement with "continuity" and "possibility." Process theologians observe this rule and reconfigure Christian doctrines accordingly. Limiting God to what is possible based on the past also requires that we redefine divine power.

Process Eschatology: A Theology of the Possible

When considering process eschatology, we must recognize its motivations. Process theologians sometimes critique more traditional Christian eschatology as being too self-centered. It's all about us, about our desire for immortality. The charge is that God becomes secondary, a kind of divine servant to the human ego. David Griffin says that the traditional belief in the resurrection of the dead is a way to guarantee that life has an ultimate meaning. Traditional belief about a decisive historical consummation of God's kingdom is a way to guarantee a final victory of good over evil. Traditional eschatology offers a solution for Christians who confront their mortality, ponder life's significance, seek final resolution for life's injustices, and want to live on after death.[10] The motivation originates with humans.

Process theology protests that reducing eschatology to human needs fails to realize that meaning is fulfilled in God, not in our individual continuation. All our "needs" are better satisfied by knowing our experiences and meaning are preserved and continue in God's life. Our immediate actions and individual selves "perish," but in God they live forever.[11] This is the process doctrine of "objective immortality" (see glossary). Immortality has not to do with my subjective "self" living on after death, but with "objective" immortality. Even though our individuality ceases (perishes) at death, its meaning and value are preserved in God's life—God's consequent nature (see glossary). Nothing is lost. In fact, as God's life is enriched, the possibilities of what God can offer the world increase. This should be sufficient.[12] Let us not selfishly make "God the means to our fulfillment."[13]

Process theologian Marjorie Suchocki charges that too often, Christians treat the reign of God as something that happens beyond this earthly life. This minimizes God's reign. By contrast, process theology emphasizes that in addition to a time to come, the reign of God involves "a judgment of the world as it is, and a call to what the world might be."[14]

But notice that Suchocki speaks of what "might" be, not what "will" be. Herein lies a problem. Unlike the hope we meet in the New Testament, neither the full reign of God nor its shape are certain. Process hope is "wishful," not "confident." God's future reign is *conditional*. What the future—including God's future—holds depends upon what results from the freedom and power of finite creatures. "God is the chief actor . . . , yet not in such a way as to eliminate the responsibility for human participation."[15]

Perhaps most problematic in all this is the process denial that God's purpose for the world, as revealed in Christ, will be concluded according to God's sovereign will. In process theology, the "dominion" of Christ is something humans can either block or cause to happen. This is not because God chooses to involve humans in his kingdom, but because God's aims cannot be achieved unless humans approve them.

A Future Without the Resurrection

As we have begun to see, for process theology, what is "reasonably possible" establishes the limits of what we can hope for in the future. This also applies to the Christian hope of the resurrection of the body. David Griffin, drawing upon John Cobb, rejects the resurrection of the body. He says the belief erroneously relies on the Hebrew belief in a soul-body unity.[16] Instead, Griffin says, we should speak of the resurrection of the soul.

Why the substitution? Why reject the hope for the resurrection of the body? Because it doesn't fit into a naturalistic "theology of the possible." Griffin is simply spelling out a conviction that governs process theology. What is observed in the natural order sets the boundaries of what can be said about God and humankind. It is not "natural" that bodies be resurrected. Whatever "life" beyond death means, it must conform to the fact that individuals perish and pass away.

Rejecting the resurrection illustrates how far process theology permits departure from the New Testament. Its underlying philosophy will not permit it to embrace an unyielding conviction of New Testament hope: salvation is for the whole person. Full conformity of Christ's people to his image will be complete only when believers are raised from the dead and conformed to Christ in the flesh just as they have already been conformed in the spirit (Rom. 8:29-30).[17] Anchored to its naturalistic philosophy, process theology is incapable of affirming with the apostle Paul that "Christ has been raised from the dead, the first fruits of those who have died" (1 Cor. 15:20), and that he is "the firstborn" of many brothers and sisters (Rom. 8:29; Col. 2:10-11; cf. 1 Cor. 15:45-49).

For the apostle Paul, the resurrection of the body has nothing to do with selfishness, as Griffin has charged. For Paul, the resurrection consummates redemption. Primarily, the Christian hope of the resurrection has to do with God's sovereign will for his people and for his creation, not primarily with what Christians desire. Process naturalism is incapable of comprehending and embracing the divine origin of Christian hope.

Not much in process theology could be more at odds with historic Christian faith and doctrine than its rejection of the resurrection of the body. Its servitude to naturalism shows how strongly bound it is to what human reason deems possible. Governed by what the world will permit, process theology is a stranger to Jesus' resurrection and the promise that his people will follow their Lord in resurrection. The process gaze is so fixed on this world that it cannot see the meaning of Christ, the new Adam—a new humanity and a new creation by the Spirit.

The Future Hope in Process Eschatology

If process theology has discarded most of traditional Christian eschatology, what does it offer instead? What is its eschatology? Like traditional Christian eschatology, process theology contains an "already" and a "not yet." The process vision of the "already" includes present liberation and wholeness. For Griffin it is possible that war, human rights violations, ecological destruction, and economic injustice will be overcome.[18] The "not yet" is confidence that values will be forever cherished in God's life. God will preserve and harmonize all values and beauty achieved in this life.

Other process theologians speak of current salvation as the reign of divine values that can overcome the demonic. Final sanctification of human life will occur in the harmonizing creativity of divine life.[19]

God's reign will come to the extent that humans respond positively to God's aims. God's reign will not result because a sovereign God bends history in conformity with some eternal plan. Obviously, that for which process theology hopes is tentative. David Griffin explains: "If a state of universal peace and happiness is ever to be realized, it will be the result of a transformation in the inner nature of the creatures and their internal relations with each other, and such a transformation cannot be imposed by God. It will be a development out of the present."[20]

God will never cease working to achieve divine aims. But God's "kingdom" will not be consummated at a point in time as the New Testament expects. No God will step forward to declare that "death will be no more; mourning and crying and pain will be no more, for the first things have passed away" (Rev. 21:4).

Marjorie Suchocki says there will never be a full overcoming of evil in human history. Overcoming evil will always be a partial human and divine project.[21] That should inspire, not discourage, us. Gradually, progress in overcoming evil may increase.[22] As progress occurs, God will be enriched. And as God is enriched, the possibilities for peace and harmony in the world increase, even though the advances are never completed under the conditions of history.[23]

Conclusion

There are instructive features of process eschatology.

First, the emphasis process theology places upon human responsibility and action can serve as a warning against laziness in God's kingdom. Misdirected Christian confidence can spawn apathy about placing ourselves in service to God's reign. Some Christians ignore those who are oppressed or marginalized while fixating on their future reward in heaven.

Second, process theology is justified in criticizing Christians who treat the Christian hope as self-serving. Many Christians forget that Christian hope loses meaning when separated from God's plan for a new humanity and a new creation. Narcissism that passes for Christian discipleship caricatures Christian hope. Reducing eschatology to our eternal bliss is idolatrous.

Third, process theology helps us remember that Christian hope loses its meaning apart from the body of Christ. Christ is redeeming a people, his church, not a bunch of isolated individuals.

Having registered these contributions, we must still conclude that what process theology means by Christian hope falls far short of what the New Testament and historic Christianity mean. They occupy two different worlds, speak of two different Gods, and describe two different forms of hope.

As important as Christian service in God's kingdom is, its consummation is not held hostage by the church, the world, or the powers and principalities arrayed against it. Assigning to finite beings the power to thwart or even retard God's plan amounts to idolatry. By contrast, the New Testament speaks of the "immeasurable greatness of [God's] power . . . put . . . to work in Christ when he raised him from the dead and seated him at his right hand in the heavenly places, far above all rule and authority and power and dominion, and above every name that is named, not only in this age but also in the age to come" (Eph. 1:19-21).

Christian hope *knows,* on the basis of God's word spoken in creation and redemption, that the one it calls Lord is the Alpha and the Omega. The kingdoms of this world will become the kingdom of our Lord, and of his Christ. He shall "reign forever and ever" (Rev. 11:15). Tethered to its naturalistic God and his inherent limitations, process theology cannot speak this confident language of Christian hope.

Chapter 12 Outline

Introduction

Reasons Why Open Theology and Process Theology Are Often Equated

Reasons Why Open Theology and Process Theology Should Not Be Equated

Open Theology, the Trinity, and Incarnation

Conclusion

12
Open Theology
Timothy J. Crutcher, Ph.D./S.T.D.

Introduction

Open theology is an important contemporary form of Christian theology. It is marked by similarities to process theology, which causes some people to place them in the same camp. But proponents of process theology reject this identification and claim that open theology belongs with orthodox Christian faith. We will examine open theology while keeping in play traditional theology and process theology.

As we have seen throughout this volume, basing process theology on process philosophy moves process theology away from the historic Christian faith. This has caused many traditional Christians to reject process theology. It has also made many leery of anything that sounds remotely similar to process theology. Though this is an understandable reaction, it can have the unfortunate result of silencing discussion of important Christian doctrines in need of careful examination.

Process theology has lodged critiques of traditional theology that merit consideration. There is, however, a big difference between *learning* from its critiques and *embracing* process theology.

Perhaps there are better ways to correct problems associated with traditional theology, ways that let us learn from criticism without departing from orthodox faith. Proponents of open theology say they offer that better way. Their proposals deal particularly with God's power and knowledge.

Some of the major proponents of open theology are Richard Rice (whose book *The Openness of God* gave the movement its name), Gregory Boyd (*God of the Possible*), Clark Pinnock (*Most Moved Mover*), and John Sanders (*The God Who Risks*).

Contrary to the charge sometimes leveled against them, open theologians are not process theologians.

Reasons Why Open Theology and Process Theology Are Often Equated

First, both affirm a strong relational understanding of God and the world. Though they express this differently, they affirm that love—persons relating to other persons—is basic to how things really are. Relationships are not just incidental by-products; they are what the world and human life are about.

Second, open theology and process theology say if the first assertion is true, then it is necessary for real freedom to exist. We cannot have true relationships without freedom. The richest relationships occur with persons who are truly other than us and whom we don't control. For example, I have no "relationship" with my left hand. It is not me, and I could survive without it. But neither is it independent enough for me to be able to "relate" to it. This is because I control it completely. It is merely an extension of me.

On the other hand, I do have a relationship with each of my children, even though they are, in one sense, extensions of me. The difference is that unlike my left hand, my children have a measure of freedom. Their freedom was rather small when they were infants. But it was still there (they cried when I tried to sleep). As they have grown, their degree of freedom and independence has also grown. Not only that, but oddly enough, the "freer" they have become, the more richly I am able to relate to them.

Process theology and open theology share this conviction about the importance of freedom for relationships. The notion that growth in freedom permits growth in relationship means that open theology and process theology are committed to a developmental or dynamic view of the world. Relationships, by their very nature, are not static. Where relationships are important, real and positive growth in freedom must be possible. A world where choices could not cause things to change for the worse or the better would be one in which true personal relationships could not form.

Third, change that involves growth in freedom has more to do with time than with space. This suggests time will play an important role in freedom and relationships for both types of theology.

Reasons Why Open Theology and Process Theology Should Not Be Equated

Open theology and process theology share the beliefs that (1) reality is relational; (2) freedom must be real; and (3) developmental change in time must be possible. They part company after this.

First, open theology aligns with traditional theology instead of process theology. It solidly bases relationships and freedom on revelation and examination of the Scriptures. Process theology first turns to reason and experience to understand relationships. Open theology turns to the Bible. For most proponents of open theology, a desire to take Scripture seriously prompted their critique of some traditional ways of talking about God. Process theology charges that traditional theology is philosophically incoherent and that it does not offer a scientifically satisfying view of God.

By contrast, open theology critiques parts of traditional theology for not accurately reflecting the Scriptures.

But there are differences between open and traditional theology on this point. Open theology challenges some traditional beliefs about God's power, his knowledge, and how God relates to time. They do this *not* because the nature of the world requires it (as with process theology) but because of how they believe God has revealed himself.

The differences between open theology and traditional theology have to do with their interpretation of Scripture and how their experiences of the world influence the way they read that book. Though the differences are important, traditional theology and open theology—unlike process theology—share a common fidelity to Scripture.

Open theology—like process theology—assigns a greater role to experience in learning how to talk about God than does some traditional theologians. But that does not make open theology any less a "revelatory theology." In the debate about whether humans can make real choices that affect the future, open theology appeals to experience that seems to show that we humans do make real choices. We are not simply playing out some predetermined script. Instead, we certainly act as if our actions affect the future. We believe that had we chosen differently in certain instances, the future would have been different.

Given that experience, when open theologians hear of situations in the Scripture where choice seems to be real ("Choose for yourselves this day whom you will serve" [Josh. 24:15]), they conclude that genuine choice is evident. In the Bible, choices are often made that cause the future to take one turn instead of another.

Some traditional theologians, on the other hand—particularly those who identify chiefly with the Augustinian-Calvinist tradition—believe the Bible teaches God's absolute determination of each event, regardless of our "experience." If one aligns with this position, then his or her perception that they act freely will not really matter. The deciding factor is what the Bible "teaches." God's sovereign control stands above our perceptions of acting freely.

The importance open theology assigns to experience is comparable to process theology. Recall, however, that process theology assigns an importance to science and makes claims about God based upon science independent of Scripture. Open theology does not do this. But it does say that if experience can play a legitimate role in how we interpret Scripture, then perhaps science also can be of assistance.

As a rule, open theology tends to be less threatened by the claims of science than some representatives of traditional theology. In discussions about the relation between science and religion, many friends of science struggle less with open theology than they do with types of traditional theology that deny real freedom. One reason is that open theology tends to assign a greater role to how the creation cooperates with God in continued creativity than do some forms of traditional theology.

Second, as we saw in chapter 2, the irreplaceable importance of revelation and Scripture for our knowledge of God establishes our belief that God transcends the world and is different from it.

Open theology affirms the same in contrast to process theology. Process theology begins with God's *natural* and *necessary* connection to the world. Open theology holds that whatever God's relationship with the world, it is purely the result of God's will. God is not embedded in and bounded by the world system as part of it and is consequently unable to stand above it.

Third, open theology and traditional theology agree there is no parity between the freedom God enjoys and freedom in God's creation.

Whereas process theologians pair God's freedom with the world's freedom as being of the same kind—just different in measure—traditional and open theology affirm God's absolute freedom. Whatever freedom the world has is contingent (dependent, finite, and therefore necessarily limited). The world is free to the extent God grants freedom to its inhabitants. God is not—indeed, cannot be—inherently bound by external constraints.

Disagreement exists between open theologians and some traditional theologians regarding God's power as it relates to human freedom. But the debate doesn't involve *whether* God is powerful. It involves what God *does with his power,* how the free God exercises power. Does God control all events, or does God grant real freedom?

The debate between process theology on the one hand, and traditional and open theology on the other is *whether* God actually has power to control events or just power to influence them. The debate is about God's essential nature.

Open and traditional theology share a common conviction about power that is not shared by process theology. For process theology, power is a "zero sum game." Decisions that involve exercising power reside either with God or with the world—not both. For process theology, God cannot use power forcefully (coercively) to control an actual occasion or any community of actual occasions. Doing so would violate the *innate* decision-making power (freedom) of the actual occasion (entity).

The process God's power is persuasive. God offers initial aims to actual occasions. There is complete freedom to accept or reject. If accepted, God subsequently acts persuasively to lure the actual occasion toward its potential.

However, if one believes in a God beyond the world who created it from nothing, then humankind's very ability to make decisions is already a *gift* from God—a result of God's creative power. God empowers humans to act freely and certainly isn't threatened by something God created.

There is debate between some traditional theologians and open theologians about freedom. Some traditional theologians deny freedom and say God created a single timeline the creation is "living out." Open theologians argue for multiple possible timelines made possible by real choices. But the debate is not about the extent of God's power and knowledge. It is about what God *has done,* not what God *can do.* The question is: What kind of world did God create: one determined in every detail, and lacking in real freedom; or one characterized by real—though limited—freedom, and consequently open to diverse futures? Whichever option one selects, each group recognizes God *could have* created the other option had God so chosen.

Fourth, if, as open theologians claim, God created a world to which he gives real freedom, then choices—be they the choices human agents make or "choices" ants make in response to a smell—actually affect the world's future. This opens the door for the important role science plays. It can explore why things happen as they do—why people get sick, how hurricanes might track—without lamely attributing everything to some predetermined plan. After all, why seek the causes of prostate cancer or river blindness if they exist because God wills it?

For open theology, the creative processes we see in nature and the creativity we see in humans—art, architecture, science—result from God's free gift. They should never be seen as competition with or rebellion against him. The gift results from the exercise of God's power. Given the world's measure of gifted creative freedom, the conflict between science and religion that sometimes shows up in traditional theology is unnecessary.

Fifth, the way open theology speaks of the world's openness differs greatly from how process theology sees things. Process theology says the world is completely open and indeterminate. God's power, and hence the future, are necessarily limited by choices the world makes. The world's freedom comes not as God's gift but because of its essential structure. Even God's future is not known until the world has its say.

Open theology, on the other hand, listens to what the Bible says about God and affirms that all freedom in the world is "bounded freedom." God is sovereign and omnipotent. He establishes the boundaries within which freedom is exercised. If God determines that a thing will happen, it will happen. Freedom given by God doesn't set aside God's sovereignty. It is, thus, incorrect to think of "open theology" as completely "open." The world is constrained by certain things God has predetermined. All human freedom is exercised in a context of finite options. For example, I can choose whether or not to eat an apple, but only because God created a world with apples. About this I have no choice at all.

Open theologians walk a middle path between some traditional theologians who say the future is already entirely predetermined, and process theology that says the future is entirely indeterminate—open even to the point of determining God's future.

The bottom line is that process theology is in a different ball park. As we saw in chapter 2, God's role in process theology is much more that of a philosophical principle than of the Holy Other One who is worthy of worship. This is not true of open theology.

Open Theology, the Trinity, and Incarnation

We can compare what open theologians are trying to do with the work of the Dutch theologian Jacob Arminius (1560-1609). Arminius objected to the hyper-Calvinism of his day (a rigid system of predestination). Open theology objects to an understanding of God that makes it difficult to worship him. Many people ask, "If we deny the reality and implications of freedom, then why claim that we make decisions for which we are religiously and morally responsible? Why bother to offer intercessory prayer if the future has already been locked up?"

We should not be surprised if some people—thinking this way about God and freedom—become disengaged. They ask, "Why bother about responsibility? Why bother with prayer? Isn't God the Great Heavenly Puppeteer who stands above the stage and pulls all the strings? What sense does it make to say that such a God 'interacts' with the world? Puppeteers don't interact; they pull strings and puppets respond accordingly."

Open theologians believe such questions are on target. They say that a puppeteer God is not the God we meet in the Scriptures. The God of the

Bible genuinely feels the creation's pain and sorrows. He is truly affected by them and in love responds.

The biblical record shows God is affected by what happens in the world. Otherwise, God's conversations with Moses, for example, would make no sense at all. Open theologians believe a God who engages the world, who takes it seriously, and who acts redemptive in spite of errant choices, elicits gratitude, love, and worship.

Open theologians believe open theology enriches our understanding of some classical Christian doctrines. One of these is the doctrine of the Trinity. A second is the incarnation. In both instances, open theologians believe they balance God's transcendence (above the world) with his immanence (in the world) more accurately than some theologies that overly stress God's transcendence, and others—process theology—that overly stress God's immanence.

The doctrine of the Trinity—a fundamental doctrine of traditional theology—affirms the dynamic and tri-personal (three persons) character of the living God. Open theology's claim regarding the relational quality of all reality is better understood when we realize that God's own life is essentially relational. Unlike process theology that founds God's relational nature upon God's relationship with the world, open theology affirms that God's relational character is inherent in his own life as God the Father, God the Son, and God the Holy Spirit.

There is little or no place for the doctrine of the Trinity in process theology, which denies "creation out of nothing." Instead, it claims that God and the world are co-eternal. They are eternally mutually dependent, and hence eternally relational. In sharp contrast, along with traditional theology, open theology affirms God's triune relational nature and the radical contingency (dependence) of the world.

Open theologians say that God's own triune life is evidenced in his relationship with the world. God's life as a relational "community of persons"—Father, Son, and Holy Spirit—is the model for his relationship with the world. God gives finite freedom to others and enables them to become "persons" in community with others and with God.

By contrast, instead of the triune God, process theology speaks of a "di-polar God." This means that that God's nature has an absolute (eternal, transcendent) "pole" and a contingent (temporal, immanent) one. As we have seen repeatedly in this volume, for process theology, God never transcends the world as he does for traditional theology. God is finally part of the world.

Christians came to believe that God is triune because he must be the kind of God who could *become* a human (incarnate) in Jesus Christ of Nazareth, even while remaining the Father whom Jesus addressed. If, as process theology teaches, God is not truly other than the world—does not truly transcend it—and hence cannot come into the world "from the outside," then the doctrines of the Trinity and incarnation make no sense at all. One could perhaps still speak of Christ as representing the creative principle of the universe. The incarnation just becomes special embodiment of something already contained in the world. But from a process perspective, claiming that the truly transcendent God became part of the world in the incarnation amounts to nonsense.

By contrast, according to open theology, by God's own free will, he came from the outside and into the world to restore freedom to those in sin. The incarnation is part of God's "re-creating," "re-giving" the gift of freedom that was his original plan. Restored freedom in humans is essential if God is to elicit the free and loving obedience God's kingdom requires.

Open theology and traditional theology may differ over just how God planned for the "Christ event," but they are solidly united regarding its centrality.

Conclusion

By comparing and contrasting open theology and process theology from numerous perspectives, we realize open theology is thoroughly orthodox. Because of this, open and process theology are in fundamentally different classes. Process theology is a philosophical theology fundamentally at odds with the historic Christian faith. Open theology reformulates some problematic aspects of traditional theology but without undermining its essential historic character.

Currently, open theology is vigorously debated. Many do not welcome its critiques of some forms of traditional theology.

Nevertheless, it is more accurate to understand the debate between traditional and open theology as a "family argument" (hardly the first time this has happened in church history) than as a debate between those who affirm historic Christian faith and those who do not. The clarification may not achieve complete resolution, but it permits us to see differences as relative rather than absolute. It ought to eliminate the emotional steam the debate often generates and permit a discussion between sisters and brothers that bears witness to the God both open theology and traditional theology worship and serve.

Chapter 13 Outline

Introduction

Why Process Theology Is Attractive

Some Weaknesses of Process Theology

Some Weaknesses of This Book

Conclusion

13

A Perfect Theology Never Existed: A Rejoinder

Thomas Jay Oord, Ph.D.

Introduction

Among all theologies of distant and recent past, none is flawless. The early church never got it perfect, and the creeds are not perfect. John Wesley's theology has flaws. No current theology is entirely satisfying, and process theology is not perfect either. "We see through a glass, darkly" (1 Cor. 13:12, KJV).

Some theologies do a better job, however, capturing core themes of the gospel. Some express better the portrait of God painted by those whom God inspired when writing the Bible. Some theologies better explain the person, message, death, and resurrection of Jesus Christ. Some support better the primary Christian commitment to love God and others as ourselves. We could list more Christian themes that some theologies address better than other theologies.

Many contemporary Christians—especially some in the Wesleyan tradition—have been attracted to process theology. Those attracted to this theology think it less flawed than most theologies. At the least, it provides important resources. Process theology has many strengths.

I am an ordained minister in the Church of the Nazarene, and I have discovered that some early leaders in my Wesleyan-oriented denomination were attracted to ideas now at the core of process theology. Those ideas appeared in a theology called personalism. Personalist scholars trained many of the early Church of the Nazarene educational leaders. One way to think of contemporary process theology is to say it carries forward the best of personalism, but in deeper conversation with science, contemporary culture, and philosophy.

Some recent theologians in my tradition find process theology helpful. In the opening pages of her influential book *A Theology of Love*, Mildred Bangs Wynkoop credits process theologian Daniel Day Williams as especially important for helping construct her book's ideas. In several publications, including *The Story of God* and *God of Nature and of Grace*, Michael Lodahl draws from process theology to argue that we best understand some issues of importance through a process theology lens.

Other Church of the Nazarene scholars and laity appreciate the process theology view of an open and not settled future. They embrace the particular understanding of God's omniscience this view entails. In the preceding chapter, Timothy Crutcher distinguishes process theology from open theology.

We could list more who find some aspects of process theology attractive. Even some in this book who write critically of process theology state their appreciation for some of its ideas.

Some critics note that process theology draws from and is largely consistent with process philosophy. They sometimes imply that theology should avoid philosophy—or at least we should not tie theology to a particular philosophy.

This implied criticism is mistaken. Philosophy of some type informs most theologies, because philosophical ideas are inescapable. Some philosophical traditions are more helpful for Bible-believing Christians than others, of course. Critics are right to worry that some philosophies undermine core themes of the broad Christian tradition.

In its proper role, philosophy is a helper. Christians should be worried, therefore, when philosophy moves from servant status to master of theology. A philosophically informed theology appeals to those who want to combine faith and reason responsibly.

Theology and its servant disciplines are like a garden with its various elements. All gardens need water, sunlight, and soil. If the soil is especially good, the garden does well. If the soil lacks proper nutrients, the garden suffers. Good philosophy is like the good soil necessary for the garden of theology. However, a good garden—not its soil—is the ultimate goal for gardeners.

Some philosophies are better resources for theology than others. Some better describe existence in general and the human condition in particular. Some philosophies are more coherent and logically consistent. Some are more applicable and practical for helping us live life well. Perhaps most importantly, some philosophies are more consonant with the broad biblical witness. Many believe process philosophy is the best philosophical resource when all of these issues are considered.

Why Process Theology Is Attractive

Contemporary Wesleyan theologians are attracted to process theology and engage the soil of its ideas—process philosophy—for good reasons. I will offer seven reasons of particular importance.

God Is Relational

Process theology offers language and ideas to support the idea that God is essentially relational. Rather than being distant, aloof, and unaffected, process theology affirms that God is present to each of us and all creation. God suffers with us all. Process theology supports the apostle Paul's words: "the God and Father of our Lord Jesus Christ, the Father of mercies and the God of all consolation, consoles us in all our affliction, so that we may be able to console those who are in any affliction with the consolation with which we ourselves are consoled by God" (2 Cor. 1:3-4). The idea that God is relational helps portray the covenantal and incarnational God the Bible describes. Although distinct from the world, God is in the world as one in whom "we live and move and have our being" (Acts 17:28).

Prayer Changes Things

Process theology argues that prayer makes a difference both to us and to God. Our prayers affect the way God chooses to act. Many biblical stories tell of how God acted differently because people prayed. Process theology supports these stories, because God as described by process theology sometimes acts differently because of what creatures do. For instance, the Lord told Isaiah to inform Hezekiah that he would die. But Hezekiah prayed that God would spare him, and God changed his mind, adding fifteen years to Hezekiah's life (Isa. 38:4-5). Other theologies cannot account for a God who changes plans because we petition. They teach that God has the past, present, and future already decided and settled. Petitionary prayer makes no difference to the God who rigidly predetermines all things. Process theology fits with the biblical revelation of a God who is influenced by our prayer.

God Made Us Free

Process theology emphasizes that we are free—at least to some degree. Our freedom is not unlimited, of course. Creaturely freedom is an important category for Wesleyans. It plays a crucial role in rejecting predestination and in placing blame for sin on creatures. Joshua understood the importance of free responses to God when he told the people, "Choose this day whom you will serve . . . but as for me and my household, we will serve the Lord" (Josh. 24:15). John Wesley called this "free grace"—God's free gift and our free response. He even sounds like a process theologian when he says, "Were human liberty taken away, men would be as incapable of virtue as stones. Therefore (with reverence be it spoken) the Almighty himself cannot do this thing. He cannot thus contradict himself or undo what he has done."[1] Overall, I know of no better conceptual scheme for affirming the Wesleyan doctrine of prevenient grace—with its view that God acts first and provides freedom to creatures for response—than the process tradition.

God Is Not Responsible for Evil

The significance of creaturely freedom, as process theology understands it, solves the problem that atheists claim remains the primary reason they cannot believe in God: the problem of evil. Process theology blames free creatures and the agency of creation for genuine evil. According to process theology, God lovingly gives freedom and therefore neither causes nor allows evil. It affirms with James, "God cannot be tempted by evil and he himself tempts no one," but that "every perfect gift is from above, coming down from the Father of lights" (1:13, 17). Process theology rejects John Calvin's idea that God is the source of Adam's sin.[2] In sum, many believe that process theology provides the best solution to the problem of evil.

Community and Individual Matter

Perhaps no theological tradition better grounds the apostle Paul's view of the church than how process theology explains the centrality of relations and community. It takes with utmost seriousness Paul's words that "we are members one of another" (Rom. 12:5). Process theologians lead the way in criticizing modern individualism, without rejecting the dignity and responsibility of persons in community. Process theology's proposal regarding interconnections and interrelatedness is important for considering what it means to be the body of Christ (1 Cor. 12:12-14). I know of no conceptual scheme that better describes how Christians are both persons and a relational community.

Contemporary Issues Must Be Engaged

Process theology engages the issues that characterize our postmodern world better than other theologies. This is especially true of contemporary science. It also deeply engages and effectively addresses environmental and ecological concerns. Process thought actively tackles the ideas of contemporary culture. Wesleyan theologians think engaging contemporary issues is crucial if Christians are to be salt and light in these wonderful and woeful days. Wesleyans and process theologians want to "always be ready to make your defense to anyone who demands from you an accounting for the hope that is in you" (1 Pet. 3:15).

Love Reigns Supreme

The previous statements represent significant reasons many in the Wesleyan tradition are attracted to process theology. However, I personally find process theology most helpful as a resource for understanding Christian love. No other theology better describes God's love as both creative and responsive. No other theology better makes sense of what Jesus called the first and second commandments (found in Matt. 22:37-40 and other Gospels). No other theology better grounds Christian *agape*. Process theology is a first-rate theology of love, and it is little wonder Mildred Bangs Wynkoop found it so helpful. If "above all," Christians should "clothe [themselves] with love" because it "binds everything together in perfect harmony" (Col. 3:14), Christians should explore the fruits of process theology.

Some Weaknesses of Process Theology

I said at the outset that no theology is perfect. Process theology has not been as strong on other topics important to Christians. In most cases, however, this weakness has less to do with process theology than with the particular interests of leading process theologians.

Just as some theologians say little about apostolic succession, environmentalism, or modern individualism, process theologians have not given as much attention as they should to some important doctrines. Essays in this book mention some of these weaknesses. Here are four more:

The Bible Is Not Always Considered Primary

The central ideas of process theology correspond well with central biblical notions about God and creation. However, I think critics rightfully request process theologians to be more explicit in their adherence to Scripture. Process theologians should attend to the Bible more closely than they typically do. It sometimes seems process theologians do not regard the Bible as principally authoritative, despite the fact that nothing in process theology prevents the Bible from retaining its pride of place in Christian theology. As someone who considers Scripture supremely authoritative for those things necessary to salvation, I think process theologians should engage the Bible more deeply and frequently.

Church Practices Need Affirmation

Recent decades have seen renewed Christian interest in what it means to be the church. For the most part, process theology has not done well in keeping up with this important trend, despite its rich relational resources. Admittedly, it has done well responding to contemporary cultural issues facing the church. In this, process theology leads the way; other theological traditions, denominations, and Christians should follow suit. However, process theologians have not done as well laying out what the role and authority of the church should be.

As far as I know, they have done little to reflect on and advocate the importance of the Eucharist and baptism. Critics are right to ask more from process theologians.

Social Ethics Are Often One-sided

Unfortunately, from my perspective, process theology has often been identified with social issues found on the liberal side of the political spectrum. This is almost entirely because most process theologians have personally embraced a liberal position on various social issues. While we all must cooperate with God to establish social justice around the world and in our own homes, liberal politics do not always support the justice needed. Although the core of process theology is neither liberal nor conservative, I believe process theology weakens itself when it identifies with one political agenda.

Christology and Trinity Require Further Exploration

Finally, I think process theologians have more work to do to develop a coherent and robust Christology and doctrine of the Trinity. To date, process theologians have done important work on Christology. Not as much has been said about the Trinity, however. Christians rightfully ask for clarification and insight into what difference process theology might make for understanding these central doctrines. Admittedly, fully "explaining" the paradox of Jesus as fully human and fully divine, and "explaining" the paradox of the Trinity as both three and one are impossible. No matter what one says about these subjects, someone will be dissatisfied.

Some Weaknesses of This Book

Some contributors to this book argue that process theology has other weaknesses. Most of these arguments do not convince me. Most of the alleged weaknesses do not pertain to core ideas of process theology. Admittedly, there are different versions of process theology, and some rightly criticize versions I, too, find inadequate. But most criticisms in this book reflect the contributors' idiosyncratic interpretations of process theology. It is fine and right for theologians to express their personal opinions. But readers should not think these opinions represent the majority view.

Careful readers will notice a great deal of disagreement among the individual writers. For instance, one essayist worries that process theology is concerned about the common good at the expense of the individual. Two other essayists argue, however, that process theology is overly concerned with the individual at the expense of the common good. Both criticisms cannot be correct, and I think both are incorrect. I think process theology offers a balanced concern for individuals, communities, and the good of the whole.

Several contributors praise process theology for making sense and being reasonable. This is one of the strengths of process theology, especially in light of the first commandment, which includes the command to love God with our minds. Yet other contributors criticize process theology for making too much sense and for being too reasonable. If God calls us to "reason together" (Isa. 1:18, NIV), it is strange to criticize a theology for being too reasonable.

One contributor rightly says that process theologians reject the idea that God has a body. Another essayist, however, says the process theologians believe God has a body. The first essayist, in this case, is correct. Process theologians tend toward the biblical language of God as Spirit (John 4:24) or John Wesley's language that God is "soul of the universe."[3] Language about the world being God's body is metaphorical, not literal.

Some contributors praise process theology for taking biblical images of God seriously and interpreting them well. I argued earlier that this is a strength of process theology, although I wish process theologians would appeal to Scripture more frequently. Other contributors, however, say process theology ignores or seriously misinterprets the Bible. These are inconsistent criticisms.

Several contributors tackle the problem of Christology, with one entire chapter devoted to the subject. Contributors rightly point out that process theology could benefit from continued exploration of how better to address christological issues. But I think process theologians are correct to say that classic Christologies presuppose an ancient philosophy no longer plausible to many contemporary people. Drawing from the philosophical categories of process philosophy will understandably mean that process Christologies sound somewhat different.

One criticism of process theology in this book is that it does not follow traditional theology closely enough. There is some truth to this claim. Process theology does not affirm everything Christians have affirmed throughout the ages. It reinterprets some Christian doctrines in light of contemporary thinking. It is wrong, however, to call process theology heretical. It is not.

I find nothing in process theology that contradicts the core themes of Christianity. It certainly asks contemporary people to think anew about what those core themes might mean. It proposes relational and event-oriented ways of thinking. These ways are sometimes at odds with the philosophies presupposed by those who wrote theology in the past. Asking Christians to think in new categories while retaining the gospel core, however, is a necessary task for any era.

The dominant philosophies supporting early Christian creeds and doctrines formulated in the Middle Ages have sometimes not done well when describing the relational God revealed in the Bible. The great commands of love and the centrality of divine love have taken a backseat to philosophical issues such as absolute sovereignty, utter transcendence, and unnecessary mystery. Classic Christian theology has often overly emphasized God as Monarch and has forgotten that God is Father and Friend. The philosophies of Athens have sometimes influenced classic Christian doctrines more than the theology of Jerusalem.

We should not ignore the important impact contemporary worldviews make on how we think about our faith. And we should not require contemporary Christians to accept ancient philosophies when contemporary ones might better support and make sense of the Christian gospel. The postmodern world in which we live deserves a theology that shows how the gospel addresses contemporary concerns. Some aspects of the classic Christian tradition reflect ancient scientific theories and worldviews that are now untenable. Change is required.

It comforts me to know that many criticisms leveled against process theology—even some in this book—are criticisms that also apply to John Wesley's theology. Some contributors might not like Wesley's thought on some theological issues. Wesley did not endorse all the ideas in the Christian tradition, predestination being one. He often appealed to the Bible in his opposition to ideas he found in conventional theology. I think his doctrine of prevenient grace would be subject to some criticisms leveled against process theology in the preceding essays. Wesley loved philosophy, engaged his culture, and read the best science of his day. Second only to the Bible, Wesley appealed to the authority of reason.[4]

Wesley was in many ways a progressive theologian. He sought to be both biblical and relevant to his time in history. In other ways, Wesley was a conservative. He called fellow Christians to return to "primitive" Christianity.

Process theology affirms both of these concerns. It seeks to retain the best of the Christian past, embrace the best of the present, and be open to the Holy Spirit's working in the future.

If the authors of the preceding essays were correct in their characterization of process theology, I would largely reject it and recommend that others do the same. In my opinion, however, significant arguments in the previous chapters do not correctly characterize process theology. A book introducing process theology would reveal that many criticisms in this book represent the particular views of the contributors, and not process theology. Most process theologians would not recognize the positions some of the essays ascribe to them.

Conclusion

In conclusion, I know of nothing in process theology that contradicts core Wesleyan-Holiness foundations or the Articles of Faith of my denomination. There are certainly differences between what some Wesleyans believe and what some process theologians believe. We should not ignore these differences. However, process theology's central claims about God's love, prevenient grace, creaturely freedom and responsibility, the person and work of Jesus Christ, the church, and so forth, fit under the Wesleyan theological umbrella.

As an open and relational theologian, I recommend that contemporary Christians carefully explore process theology for themselves. I recommend that they seek to discover through prayer and reflection whatever fruit process theology might offer. We can find some aspects of process theology helpful without endorsing everything it proposes. I take that approach to process theology and other theological proposals. I try to combine charitable openness and careful discernment, and I encourage other Christians to do the same.

Before accepting wholeheartedly what any of us have said, I urge readers to consult introductions to process theology. I recommend John B. Cobb Jr., *The Process Perspective: Frequently Asked Questions About Process Theology*, and Robert Mesle, *Process Theology: A Basic Introduction*. I urge you, your friends, and your community to seek to hear the full story.

I began this essay by claiming that a perfect theology has never existed. I join contributors to this book by agreeing that process theology has its flaws. All theologies have flaws. However, I hope the foregoing explains why some in the Wesleyan tradition and in my own denomination find process theology attractive.

As we seek always to be ready to give an account for our Christian hope, let us wisely seek language, ideas, and practices that—despite their flaws and limitations—help us respond well to Jesus' call to love God and our neighbors as ourselves. Let us listen closely to the church. Let us use our reason and reflect on our experience. Above all, let us be led by the Holy Spirit as we explore the Bible.

For at present "we see through a glass, darkly." Only later will we see "face to face." We now "know in part." Despite our not knowing in full, we rejoice that we are fully known (1 Cor. 13:12, KJV).

Amen.

Conclusion

"Promise" or "peril"? Isn't that the question the church has historically asked of those who want to interpret its faith for a new generation or era? In its Scriptures and creeds the church has found more than adequate norms for assessing candidates. In each succeeding era the church has had to decide whether its faith will continue to be defined and governed by those norms or by new ones. Never has the church been more tempted to alter its norms than today.

Process theology offers itself to the church as a "promise," not as a "peril." Fine. Then let it answer the following: Will it submit all it offers to strict governance by the Scriptures and the creeds? Will it submit to a close reading of the Scriptures and the faith's rich and often perilous history? Most importantly, will it submit wholly and unreservedly to the Immanuel God, God incarnate, who said, "Take My yoke upon you and learn from Me, for I am gentle and lowly in heart, and you will find rest for your souls. For My yoke is easy and My burden is light" (Matt. 11:29, NKJV)? Does it recognize in him the definitive and conclusive self-disclosure of the Father? In the Risen One, does it encounter the thrice holy God?

If with the church through the ages, process theology will answer "Yes!" "*Credo!*" then the church can justifiably embrace its "promise." Let it take a seat at the apostolic table. If it cannot, then no matter how similar its language might at times be to the language of Zion, it must be rejected, just as have other suitors such as Gnosticism, Arianism, and Enlightenment revisionism.

In his pivotal 1520 writing about the Sacraments—*The Babylonian Captivity of the Church*—Martin Luther stated succinctly what has been settled in orthodox Christian faith for more than 1,500 years. In Jesus Christ, God in full deity, and human in full humanity "are present in their entirety." Luther added, we can "appropriately say: 'This man is God'; or, 'This God is man.' Though philosophy cannot grasp it, yet faith can. The authority of the word of God goes beyond the capacity of our mind."[1]

Today, thanks to the excellent scholarship of such New Testament scholars as Luke Timothy Johnson and N. T. Wright, and a careful reading of the creeds offered by a host of faithful scholars, our reasons for making Luther's confession are stronger than ever. And our tools for raising and answering the question, Promise or peril? of all theologies are sharper. It remains our inescapable responsibility to become acquainted with them and to employ them carefully. Error in answering the question will not occur for lack of good ways to question.

In this volume, charges have been made that process theology depends upon a philosophy that necessarily rules out the Christian confession that in Jesus of Nazareth we definitively encounter Immanuel—for all ages and all peoples. The contributors who draw this conclusion believe the scales tilt heavily in the direction of peril. Tom Oord has argued to the contrary. He believes the scales tilt heavily in the direction of promise.

The "proof of the pudding will be in the eating." Observers must carefully examine what the contributors have said, the language process theologians use, what they include and omit, and what the New Testament says about Jesus Christ, his heavenly Father, and the Holy Spirit. Go further. Read the process theologians while also reading such introductions to the New Testament as *The Writings of the New Testament* by Luke T. Johnson,[2] or presentations of Jesus like *The Challenge of Jesus* by N. T. Wright,[3] and expositions of the creeds such as Karl Barth's treatment of the Apostles' Creed in *Dogmatics in Outline*.[4] Then ask, "Does process theology 'hold fast to the confession of our hope without wavering'?" (Heb. 10:23, NRSV).

After all discussions are concluded—whether theological or philosophical—the unshakable confession of Christian faith remains: in Jesus of Nazareth, obedient faith encounters God in God's fullness (Col. 1:15-20) and humanity in human fullness (John 1:14). Incarnate, this is the Son of God through whom the Father created and redeems all things by the power of the Holy Spirit—God Triune forever.

Let there be no mistake. For the church through the ages, the crucifixion of Jesus is his moment of glorification and the definitive revelation of God's glory (John 3:14-15; 8:28; 11:4). "Now is the judgment of this world; now the ruler of this world will be driven out. And I, if I am lifted up from the earth, will draw all people to myself" (12:31-32). This very Jesus, and none other, is Lord (1:23), temple (2:17), the living bread come down from heaven (6:31, 45), Son of God (10:36), and king (12:13, 15). He is the *fulfillment* of the Scriptures (19:30; "accomplished," *tetelestai*).

Either by grace and faith we make this confession without equivocation, or we surrender any justifiable reason to call ourselves or our theologies or our denominations or our philosophies "Christian." The New Testament and church history chronicle failed efforts to hedge and modify the confession. They have failed and will forever fail because the church and its confession belong to and are shepherded by the crucified, risen, and reigning Christ.

"And did those feet in ancient time walk upon Israel's mountains green?
And did the Christ of heaven come down?
Was God in flesh both heard and seen? And did He die to prove His love?
And did He rise more pow'rful still?
And was His rule on earth started there upon Golgotha's tragic hill?
Bring me my bow of burning gold!
Bring me my arrows of desire! Bring me my spear!
O clouds unfold! Bring me my chariots of fire!
I will not cease to spread His light: my faith a shield,
His word my sword; 'til Christ, my God, is crowned as King,
and all the earth shall own Him Lord."
(C. Hubert H. Parry, 1848-1918)

Appendixes

Appendix A
Glossary of Process Terms

A basic explanation: Process philosophy attempts to explain the *developmental* nature of reality. It emphasizes *becoming* rather than static existence or being. It also stresses the interrelatedness of all entities. Process describes reality as ultimately made up of experiential events rather than enduring inert substances.

Actual Entity: Alfred Whitehead (1861-1947) says that "the actual world is a process, and the process is the becoming of actual entities. At its most fundamental level the world is made up of momentary events of experience instead of enduring material substances. These momentary events are called 'actual occasions' or 'actual entities.' They are essentially self-determining, experiential, and internally related to each other.

"Actual entities are creatures; they are also termed 'actual occasions.'"[1] An actual entity "is the real concrescence of many potentials."[2] Whitehead says that *actual entity* and *actual occasion* can be used interchangeably. But Marjorie Hewitt Suchocki says that actual entity should be reserved for God. She says that while actual occasions occupy the spatio-temporal realm, God in his primordial nature does not.

When an actual entity achieves its completion (satisfaction) it "perishes" and becomes potential data for a subsequent actual entity in the process of becoming.

Actual Occasion: Each unit of process is called an actual occasion or actual entity. Actual occasions are the building blocks of the universe. They are bursts of energy (drops of experience). Each one comes into being and fades away in a split second. Actual occasions are the final building blocks that make up the composite world of rocks, trees, and people. Whitehead called them energy events or actual occasions of experience.

    A. Each energy event has a physical pole and a mental pole.
        1. The physical pole is that aspect which is purely a repeat of past energy events.

2. The mental pole is an element of subjectivity and, therefore, of limited but genuine freedom that enables the energy event, in the process of becoming, to have some determination over the shape it will take, and to receive new possibilities from God, the initial aim.
B. God and our spirits or souls are each a series of these energy events that are highly developed in complexity, especially in regard to the mental pole.

Concrescence: Concrescence describes the succession of phases by which actual occasions come to exist and achieve "satisfaction." It is the activity of becoming. Whitehead speaks of a "concrescence [integration] of prehensions."[3] Concrescence names the "production of novel togetherness."[4] It unites many feelings into one actual occasion. This requires that the past be evaluated and selectively chosen for the new concrescing (emerging) event (occasion).

Concrescence is the self-production of the subject. It exhibits creativity in the process of becoming actual. The completed process will constitute the event's "satisfaction." It will then exercise "transitional creativity" by influencing the becoming of a subsequent occasion.

"Creation," the: Process philosophy rejects the doctrine of creation ex nihilo (creation out of nothing). Process is eternal. While our universe had a temporal beginning, universes have existed previously and will exist after ours. God has always been *with* the world in some form. While there is a final end to our universe, there is no final end to creation as such.

Creativity: Creativity is the ultimate category or concept in process philosophy. It is "the universal of universals characterizing ultimate matter of fact. It is the ultimate principle by which the many, which are the universe disjunctively, become the one actual occasion, which is the universe conjunctively." Creativity is "the principle of novelty."[5] From the principle of creativity all other parts of the process system proceed. This includes God. "God is [the] primordial, non-temporal accident [expression]" of creativity.[6] Creativity is the ultimate metaphysical category, the foundation of reality. It is not a "thing" or "being." Creativity becomes actual "in virtue of its accidents."[7]

Dipolar Theism: Charles Hartshorne (1897-2000), one of Whitehead's students, advanced a form of process philosophy known as dipolar theism and neoclassical theism (a rational, philosophical statement of God's existence).

Appendix A

While God's essence remains unchanging, God's existence changes in relationship with the world. The "pole" of God's nature remains eternally constant; the "pole" of God's experience everlastingly changes in interaction with others. The neoclassical alternative is to speak of God as dipolar. God is in different respects finite and infinite, temporal and eternal, complex and simple, contingent and noncontingent. Only when including both poles can we speak of God's perfection. Hartshorne said that classical theism saw God as void of suffering. God is impassible, which means that in his perfection he is incapable of feeling pain, of suffering the world's sufferings, of feeling.

Eternal Objects: Eternal objects are pure possibilities (potentialities) for becoming definite. They reside in God's primordial nature. God offers them to becoming entities (occasions) as their initial aim or direction for becoming. Whitehead says that eternal objects "can be described only in terms of their potential for 'ingression' into the becoming of actual entities."[8]

God's Consequent Nature: Whitehead called God's experience God's "consequent nature" (physical pole). God is continually affected and influenced by the world. The consequent nature results as God "feels" (experiences) the world and transforms the "feelings" into an ever-deeper unity and harmony. God's consequent nature derives from God in his primordial nature having offered achievable aims to the world, and from the world's creative achievement of those aims.

God's Power: God's power is persuasive (calling energy events forward through the initial aim) and not coercive. To persuade is to seek to work together with others, rather than entirely controlling others (coercion). God's persuasion has been able to bring forth this magnificent creation. God has the power needed to profoundly affect and shape the universe, and to inspire awe and worship in us.

God's Primordial Nature: God's primordial nature (mental pole) comprehensively contains the pure possibilities (aims) that God can offer to the world of actual occasions. It is that aspect of God that deals with novel possibilities. God's circumstantial will arises out of God's primordial nature (mental pole). It is circumstantial because God's consequent nature (physical pole) is constantly being enriched and modified by what occurs in the world. What happens in the world affects God's primordial nature; on that basis

God adjusts the possibilities (aims) that would be best to offer at any given moment and place.

Initial Aim: The initial aim inaugurates the becoming of a new occasion. It originates in God's primordial nature. God's knowledge of the emerging actual occasion's entire past—what it has achieved and failed to achieve with reference to God's goal for it, and its own subjective aim—is integrated with God's own purposes. This yields a particular possibility for what the new occasion might become. God offers the possibility to the occasion as its initial aim. The initial aim presents the optimum way for the actual occasion to unify the many influences it receives from its past.

Metaphysics: In this book, the more traditional meaning of the term is used. It names the study of the *first principles* or *first causes* of reality or things. It studies the causes that lie behind the physical and the phenomenal and delineates between "essence" (substance) and "accident." Process philosophy, or the "philosophy of organism" as Whitehead calls it in *Process and Reality*,[9] proceeds according to the traditional understanding of metaphysics.

Whitehead identifies metaphysics traditionally as the examination of "the ultimate," which becomes "actual in virtue of its accidents."[10] The "ultimate" is rationally engaged (known) and mapped with reference to itself and its concrete manifestations. Although theology may utilize metaphysics, metaphysics is a philosophical enterprise, not a religious one. The traditional definition of metaphysics is no longer accepted by some philosophers, in part because some philosophers doubt that the traditional goal is possible.

Objective Immortality: Whitehead says that in the philosophy of organism actual entities "perpetually perish" as subjects upon their "satisfaction" (completion). But they are immortal objectively. In perishing, actual entities lose their subjective immediacy but they acquire objectivity—efficient causation for subsequent entities.[11]

Marjorie Hewitt Suchocki explains that objective immortality refers to how an actual occasion affects its successors. "The effect is the transmission of its own value to another by way of transitional creativity. There can be both repetitive and transformative elements in immortality." All completed entities affect their successors in some measure. "The more complex entities, however, can also anticipate their own participation in some wider scheme of things, and hence become a force for transformation through objective immortality. The process is objective, since no finite occasion can prehend another in its entirety. The other is felt as object. This process is termed immortality, since it perpetuates one's continuing effect through the universe."[12]

Personalism: Personalism is a philosophy that developed in the nineteenth century and achieved special designation as a philosophy in the first half of the twentieth century. The title is properly applicable to any school of thought that concentrates on the reality of persons and their unique status among beings in general. Because personalism existed in diverse forms, it is difficult to define as a philosophical and theological movement. Some speak of *personalisms*. The most important common feature of personalism is its affirmation of the centrality of the person for philosophical thought. Personalism sees ultimate reality and value as residing in personhood—human and divine. The significance, uniqueness, and inviolability of the person are central. Persons are essentially relational or communitarian. The title can therefore legitimately be applied to any school of thought that focuses on the reality of persons and their unique status among beings in general.

Prehension: Prehension refers to the initial process by which the emergent actual occasion appropriates ("feels") the relevant past for its own novel becoming. Prehension is a phase of concrescence. The particular character of every event, and consequently the world, results from a selective process in which the relevant past is creatively brought together to become the new event. Prehension is an essential phase of creative advance as many past events are integrated in the events of the present. When the process is complete the result will in turn be taken up (prehended) by future events. The universe proceeds as "the many become one, and are increased by one" in a sequence of integrations at every level and moment of existence.

Process philosophy distinguishes between a positive and negative prehension. "Positive" refers to a becoming actual occasion *choosing* to incorporate past data. "Negative" refers to a becoming occasion *rejecting* past data as relevant (constitutive) for its becoming. "Physical prehension" refers to the prehension of "satisfied" (completed) actual entities. "Conceptual prehension" refers to the prehension of eternal objects.[13]

Process: Whitehead says "the actual world is a process" and the "process is the becoming of actual entities. Thus actual entities are creatures; they are also termed 'actual occasions.'"[14] Process is the becoming (or "taking shape") of energy events and is determined by three factors.

- Past energy events (cause and effect) influence present energy events (at the physical pole) as they take shape.
- God, through the giving of the initial aim, influences the shaping of present energy events at the mental pole, which is the pole that receives and considers novelty.
- The subjectivity (and therefore freedom or partial self-determination) of the mental pole of energy events in the process of becoming significantly effects the shapes these events take.

Process Philosophy: Process philosophy applies the work of Alfred North Whitehead and Charles Hartshorne to standard philosophical problems. Process thought seeks to integrate and reconcile the diverse facets of human experience (i.e., ethical, religious, aesthetic, and scientific intuitions) into one coherent explanatory scheme. The most common applications of process thought are in the fields of philosophy and theology. However, process has also found a meaningful foothold in many other discussions, including ecology, economics, physics, biology, education, psychology, feminism, and cultural studies. A major vehicle for this is the journal *Process Studies*.[15]

In spite of the systematic character of process philosophy (a "philosophy of organism"), Alfred N. Whitehead expressed an admirable modesty about his efforts. "Philosophy has been haunted by the unfortunate notion that its method is dogmatically to indicate premises which are severally clear, distinct, and certain; and to erect upon those premises a deductive system of thought. . . . an accurate expression of the final generalities is the goal [the philosophy or organism] and not its origin."[16]

Process Theology: Interprets doctrines in Christianity and other world religions in terms of the relational worldview generated by Whitehead and later developers of his work.

Satisfaction: Satisfaction is the final phase of concrescence.

Societies of Occasions: What we ordinarily call individuals, the sorts of things that endure through time, are actually "societies" of individuals. "Personal human existence is a 'serially ordered society' of [actual] occasions of experience."[17]

Subjective Aim: The subjective aim controls the becoming of a subject (actual entity or actual occasion). It is the subject accepting or rejecting, with purpose, the antecedent data, including the initial aim, offered for adoption (prehension).

Superject: Whitehead says that the complete term for a becoming actual entity is subject-superject. A subject (actual entity) in the process of becoming is at once the subject experiencing and the superject, namely, something for others—for subsequent actual entities. The term "subject" is reserved for an actual entity's own real constitution. "But subject is always to be construed as an abbreviation of 'subject-superject.'"[18]

Temporality: Temporality is the process of transition from actual occasion to actual occasion. The actual occasions of which the temporal process is composed are themselves processes of momentary becoming, their "concrescence," their becoming concrete.

The definitions in this glossary are composed of material drawn from Alfred N. Whitehead, *Process and Reality: An Essay in Cosmology* (1978); the web site of the Center for Process Studies, http://ctr4process.org/about/general.shtml; John B. Cobb Jr. and David Ray Griffin, *Process Theology: An Introduction*; Marjorie Hewitt Suchocki, *God, Christ, Church*, 257-59; and *The Internet Encyclopedia of Philosophy,* http://www.iep.utm.edu/processp/.

Appendix B

The Creeds

The Nicene Creed (A.D. 325) (Nicaeno-Constantinopolitan Creed, A.D. 381)

We believe in one God,
the Father, the Almighty,
of all that is, seen and unseen.

We believe in one Lord, Jesus Christ,
the only Son of God,
eternally begotten of the Father,
God from God, Light from Light,
true God from true God,
begotten, not made,
of one Being with the Father.
Through him all things were made.
For us and for our salvation
he came down from heaven:
by the power of the Holy Spirit
he became incarnate from the Virgin Mary,
and was made man.
For our sake he was crucified under Pontius Pilate;
he suffered death and was buried.
On the third day he rose again
in accordance with the Scriptures;
he ascended into heaven
and is seated at the right hand of the Father.
He will come again in glory to judge the living and the dead,
and his kingdom will have no end.
We believe in the Holy Spirit, the Lord, the giver of life,
who proceeds from the Father and the Son.
With the Father and the Son he is worshipped and glorified.
He has spoken through the Prophets.
We believe in one holy catholic and apostolic Church.
We acknowledge one baptism for the forgiveness of sins.
We look for the resurrection of the dead,
and the life of the world to come. Amen.

The Definition of the Council of Chalcedon (A.D. 451)

Therefore, following the holy fathers, we all with one accord teach men to acknowledge one and the same Son, our Lord Jesus Christ, at once complete in Godhead and complete in manhood, truly God and truly man, consisting also of a reasonable soul and body; of one substance with the Father as regards his Godhead, and at the same time of one substance with us as regards his manhood; like us in all respects, apart from sin; as regards his Godhead, begotten of the Father before the ages, but yet as regards his manhood begotten, for us men and for our salvation, of Mary the Virgin, the God-bearer; one and the same Christ, Son, Lord, Only-begotten, recognized in two natures, without confusion, without change, without division, without separation; the distinction of natures being in no way annulled by the union, but rather the characteristics of each nature being preserved and coming together to form one person and subsistence, not as parted or separated into two persons, but one and the same Son and Only-begotten God the Word, Lord Jesus Christ; even as the prophets from earliest times spoke of him, and our Lord Jesus Christ himself taught us, and the creed of the fathers has handed down to us.

The Apostles' Creed

I believe in God, the Father Almighty,
> the Maker of heaven and earth,
> and in Jesus Christ, His only Son, our Lord:

Who was conceived by the Holy Ghost,
> born of the virgin Mary,
> suffered under Pontius Pilate,
> was crucified, dead, and buried;

He descended into hell.
The third day He arose again from the dead;
He ascended into heaven,
> and sitteth on the right hand of God the Father Almighty;
> from thence he shall come to judge the quick and the dead.

I believe in the Holy Ghost;
> the holy catholic church;
> the communion of saints;
> the forgiveness of sins;
> the resurrection of the body;
> and the life everlasting.

Amen.

Athanasian Creed

(The creed is of uncertain origin. Traditionally is has been attributed to fourth century Athanasius of Alexandria, but many scholars place its origin in the fifth or sixth centuries. The creed communicates two essential points: (1) that God's Son and the Holy Spirit are of one being with the Father; and (2) that Jesus Christ is true God and true man in one person. Traditionally it is considered the "Trinitarian Creed.")

Whoever wants to be saved should above all cling to the catholic faith.
Whoever does not guard it whole and inviolable will doubtless perish eternally.
Now this is the catholic faith: We worship one God in trinity and the Trinity in unity, neither confusing the persons nor dividing the divine being.
For the Father is one person, the Son is another, and the Spirit is still another.
But the deity of the Father, Son, and Holy Spirit is one, equal in glory, coeternal in majesty.
What the Father is, the Son is, and so is the Holy Spirit.
Uncreated is the Father; uncreated is the Son; uncreated is the Spirit.
The Father is infinite; the Son is infinite; the Holy Spirit is infinite.
Eternal is the Father; eternal is the Son; eternal is the Spirit: And yet there are not three eternal beings, but one who is eternal; as there are not three uncreated and unlimited beings, but one who is uncreated and unlimited.
Almighty is the Father; almighty is the Son; almighty is the Spirit: And yet there are not three almighty beings, but one who is almighty.
Thus the Father is God; the Son is God; the Holy Spirit is God: And yet there are not three gods, but one God.
Thus the Father is Lord; the Son is Lord; the Holy Spirit is Lord: And yet there are not three lords, but one Lord.
As Christian truth compels us to acknowledge each distinct person as God and Lord, so catholic religion forbids us to say that there are three gods or lords.
The Father was neither made nor created nor begotten; the Son was neither made nor created, but was alone begotten of the Father; the Spirit was neither made nor created, but is proceeding from the Father and the Son.

Thus there is one Father, not three fathers; one Son, not three sons; one Holy Spirit, not three spirits.

And in this Trinity, no one is before or after, greater or less than the other; but all three persons are in themselves, coeternal and coequal; and so we must worship the Trinity in unity and the one God in three persons.

Whoever wants to be saved should think thus about the Trinity.

It is necessary for eternal salvation that one also faithfully believe that our Lord Jesus Christ became flesh.

For this is the true faith that we believe and confess: That our Lord Jesus Christ, God's Son, is both God and man.

He is God, begotten before all worlds from the being of the Father, and he is man, born in the world from the being of his mother—existing fully as God, and fully as man with a rational soul and a human body; equal to the Father in divinity, subordinate to the Father in humanity.

Although he is God and man, he is not divided, but is one Christ.

He is united because God has taken humanity into himself; he does not transform deity into humanity.

He is completely one in the unity of his person, without confusing his natures.

For as the rational soul and body are one person, so the one Christ is God and man.

He suffered death for our salvation. He descended into hell and rose again from the dead.

He ascended into heaven and is seated at the right hand of the Father.

He will come again to judge the living and the dead.

At his coming all people shall rise bodily to give an account of their own deeds.

Those who have done good will enter eternal life, those who have done evil will enter eternal fire.

This is the catholic faith.

One cannot be saved without believing this firmly and faithfully.

Notes

Introduction

1. David C. Steinmetz, "Calvin as Biblical Interpreter Among the Ancient Philosophers," *Interpretation* 63, no. 2 (April 2009): 142-53.

2. John Wesley, "Sermons on Several Occasions: First Series," preface, par. 5, (1771), http://www.tparents.org/Library/Religion/Christian/Wesley/preface.html (accessed April 15, 2010).

3. Albert C. Outler, *Theology in the Wesleyan Spirit* (Nashville: Discipleship Resources-Tidings, 1975), 5.

4. D. Stephen Long, *John Wesley's Moral Theology: The Quest for God and Goodness* (Nashville: Kingswood Books, 2005), 45.

5. Outler, *Theology in the Wesleyan Spirit*, 5.

6. Ibid., 6.

7. Long, *John Wesley's Moral Theology*, 45.

8. Outler, *Theology in the Wesleyan Spirit*, 5.

9. Schubert M. Ogden, *The Reality of God* (New York: Harper and Row, Publishers, 1977), 190.

10. Hartshorne (1897-2000) said that "classical theism" treated God's love as "unsympathetic goodness," meaning that God's love for us is an "unsympathetic" love. He charged that "classical theism" presented God as one who does not "rejoice with us, is not made happy by our joy or good fortune [and is not] grieved by our sorrow or misery" (*Omnipotence and Other Theological Mistakes* [Albany, NY: State Univ. of New York, 1984], 4). The term "neoclassical theism" is often used to describe the concept of God process philosophy supports. Hartshorne was its chief representative. "Neoclassical theism" opposes what Hartshorne calls "classical theism (the one too strongly influenced by Greek philosophy as medieval scholars knew that philosophy" [ibid., 1]). Hartshorne equated the following terms: "new theism," "Process theology," and "neoclassical theism." He worked principally as a philosopher, not as a Christian theologian. The current book deals more narrowly with distinct Christian uses of process philosophy.

11. Jurgen Moltmann, *The Crucified God: The Cross of Christ as the Foundation and Criticism of Christian Theology* (London: SCM Press Ltd, 1982).

12. Colin E. Gunton, *Becoming and Being: The Doctrine of God in Charles Hartshorne and Karl Barth* (Oxford: Oxford Univ. Press, 1980), 139-48.

13. "Process theology operates on the one side from the perspective of Christian faith and on the other in the metaphysical context provided by process philosophy and its doctrine of God" (John B. Cobb Jr. and David Ray Griffin, *Process Theology: An Introductory Exposition* [Philadelphia: Westminster Press, 1976], 41).

14. Ibid., 14.

15. Marjorie Hewitt Suchocki, *God, Christ, Church: A Practical Guide to Process Theology* (New York: Crossroad, 1989), 82.

16. John B. Cobb Jr., *Reclaiming the Church: Where the Mainline Churches Went Wrong and What to Do About It* (Louisville, KY: Westminster/John Knox Press, 1997), 101.

17. Cobb and Griffin, *Process Theology*, 43.

18. Suchocki, *God, Christ, Church*, 45.

19. Marjorie Hewitt Suchocki, "What Is Process Theology? A Conversation with Marjorie," http://www.processandfaith.org/publications/RedBook/What%20Is%20Process%20 Theology.pdf. The Center for Process Studies http://www.ctr4process.org/about/process/.

By using the particular understanding of reality as formulated by philosopher Alfred North Whitehead, "We push toward the rewards of communicating Christian faith in thought forms that reflect a contemporary understanding of reality" (*God, Christ, Church,* 4). Suchocki demonstrates how effectively this can be done in her penetrating discussion of original sin, societal evil, and the demonic in chapter 2 of *God, Christ, Church.*

20. Process theology is also referred to as "process theism."

21. Gunton quotes Lutheran theologian Robert W. Jenson as saying, "The trouble with process theology is that it is such an attractive alternative to the Christian faith." Jenson is himself quoting an unnamed colleague (Robert Jenson, *God After God: The God of the Past and the God of the Future, Seen in the Work of Karl Barth* [Bel Air, CA: Bobbs-Merrill Co., 1969], 208). Gunton raises the possibility that process theology is actually a competitor to the Christian faith (216).

22. The Center for Process Studies provides a wealth of information regarding process thought and theology. http://www.ctr4process.org/

23. Cobb, *Reclaiming the Church.*

24. Suchocki, *God, Christ, Church,* 153.

Chapter 2

1. Charles Hartshorne, *Creative Synthesis and Philosophic Method* (Chicago: Open Court, 1970), xviii.

2. A good example of this is David Ray Griffin, *A Process Christology* (Lanham, MD: University Press of America, 1990).

3. See Dan Dombrowski, "Charles Hartshorne" in online *Stanford Encyclopedia of Philosophy,* http://plato.stanford.edu/entries/hartshorne/ (accessed September 10, 2009).

4. Hartshorne, *Omnipotence and Other Theological Mistakes,* 58.

5. John B. Cobb and Franklin I. Gamwell, eds., *Existence and Actuality: Conversations with Charles Hartshorne* (Chicago: Univ. of Chicago Press, 1984), 124.

Chapter 3

1. Charles Taylor, *A Secular Age* (Cambridge, MA: Belknap Press of Harvard Univ. Press, 2007), 351.

2. David Ray Griffin helpfully uses this term to describe process philosophy's view of God. See David Ray Griffin, *Reenchantment Without Supernaturalism: A Process Philosophy of Religion* (Ithaca, NY: Cornell Univ. Press, 2001), especially 129-48.

3. Ibid., 473-504.

4. Russell Pregeant, "Scripture and Revelation," in *Handbook of Process Theology,* eds. Jay B. McDaniel and Donna Bowman (St. Louis: Chalice Press, 2006), 67.

5. This is abundantly clear in John Cobb, *Christ in a Pluralistic Age* (Philadelphia: Westminster Press, 1975), and Suchocki, *God, Christ, Church.*

6. Donna Bowman, "God for Us: A Process View of the Divine-Human Relationship," in *Handbook of Process Theology,* 12.

7. William A. Beardslee, et al., *Biblical Preaching on the Death of Jesus* (Nashville: Abingdon Press, 1989), 41.

8. Ibid.

Chapter 4

1. At this point I must introduce a technical point. Process theology believes that the universe in some form is everlasting, with no beginning and no end. However, it understands that the universe in its current form—with its current configuration of matter, energy, space, time, and laws—has not always existed. The universe in its current form had

(scientists believe) a beginning and may well have an end. But for process theology, the current form of the universe, even if it lasts billions and billions of years, is only a portion of the long history of the universe. It is the universe in this latter sense that exists everlastingly, without beginning and without end.

Chapter 5

1. Cobb and Griffin, *Process Theology*, 104.
2. Bowman, "God for Us," 14-15.
3. Ibid.
4. Norman Pittenger, *The Only Meaning* (Oxford: A. R. Mowbray and Co., 1969), 126.
5. Ibid., 112. See also, John B. Cobb Jr., *The Process Perspective: Frequently Asked Questions About Process Theology*, ed. Jeanyne B. Slettom (St. Louis: Chalice Press, 2003), 22: "We use what understanding of love we have in ordinary life, especially our experience of healthy parental love, and we affirm that we discern the perfect embodiment of this in God."
6. Cobb and Griffin, *Process Theology*, 105. See also Suchocki, *God, Christ, Church*, 91.
7. Schubert M. Ogden, *The Reality of God and Other Essays* (New York: Harper and Row, 1966), 177.
8. This is what I take to be the chief insight of the traditional doctrine of the hypostatic union, the idea that Jesus happens as the divine and human natures are united in one person, the eternal Logos of God.
9. C. Robert Mesle, *Process Theology: A Basic Introduction* (St. Louis: Chalice Press, 1993), 106-7.
10. Norman Pittenger, *The Word Incarnate: A Study in the Doctrine of the Person of Christ* (New York: Harper and Brothers, 1959), 221.
11. Cobb and Griffin, *Process Theology*, 102.
12. Language about the life of Christ exemplifying a fully human "supreme ideal" is adapted from Alfred North Whitehead. See Alfred North Whitehead, *Religion in the Making* (New York: Macmillan, 1926), 57.
13. Norman Pittenger, *Unbounded Love: God and Men in Process* (New York: Seabury Press, 1976), 11.
14. Cobb, *Process Perspective*, 37.
15. At this point particularly, process Christology perhaps most clearly shows itself to be a species of Arianism. The essential Arian error is not just in saying that Christ is a creature who is "like God" (though that is problematic), but in a dissociation of "Jesus" from the identity of God as such, and its placing of Jesus in some more universal definition of *being*, determined by the fashionable metaphysical categories of the time.
16. See John B. Cobb Jr., *Christ in a Pluralistic Age* (Louisville, KY: Westminster/John Knox Press, 1999), 203-20.
17. Ibid., 66.
18. See Robert B. Mellert, *What Is Process Theology?* (New York: Paulist Press, 1978), 78.
19. Cobb, *Process Perspective*, 40.

Chapter 6

1. N. T. Wright, *Justification* (Downers Grove, IL: IVP Academic, 2009), 34.
2. The fourth century Visigoths—conquerors of the Iberian Peninsula—were Arians. They converted to Nicene orthodoxy in the late sixth century.
3. Although orthodoxy "honors and accepts" the teaching of the Athanasian and Apostles' Creeds, they don't have the importance Roman Catholics and Protestants assign to them. "They have not been proclaimed by an Ecumenical Council." Timothy Ware, *The Orthodox Church* (New York: Penguin Books, 1978), 210.

4. Ibid.

5. St. Augustine, "A Sermon to Catechumens on the [Apostles'] Creed."

6. Brian Davies, *The Thought of Thomas Aquinas* (Oxford: Clarendon Paperbacks, 1993), 274-76.

7. Thomas Aquinas, *On the Power of God,* Question X: The Procession of the Divine Persons; Article IV: Does the Holy Spirit Proceed From the Son? 24. *Reply to the Thirteenth Objection.*

8. Martin Luther, "An Appeal to the Ruling Class of German Nationality as to the Amelioration of the State of Christendom," Section III, 1520, *Martin Luther: Selections from His Writings,* ed. John Dillenberger (Garden City, NY: Anchor Books, 1961), 433, 467.

9. Ibid., "Sermons of the Catechism: The [Apostles'] Creed," 1528, 209-14.

10. John Calvin, *The Institutes of the Christian Religion,* Book IV, chapter 9, section 8.

11. Ibid.

12. John Wesley, "A Letter to a Roman Catholic," *John Wesley,* ed. Albert C. Outler (New York: Oxford Univ. Press, 1964), 494-95.

13. Marjorie Hewitt Suchocki refers to Christian process theology as "process-relational" theology.

14. Suchocki, *God, Christ, Church,* 5.

15. John B. Cobb Jr., *God and the World* (Philadelphia: Westminster Press, 1969), 47.

16. Colin E. Gunton, *The Triune Creator: A Historical and Systematic Study* (Grand Rapids: Eerdmans, 1998), 8-11.

17. Ibid., 8-11.

18. Suchocki, *God, Christ, Church,* 68. God is bipolar: a "mental pole" and a "physical pole," referring to God's "feeling" of completed actualities and to God's "feeling" of possibilities, respectively.

19. Ibid., 80.

20. Richard B. Hays, *The Moral Vision of the New Testament: A Contemporary Introduction to New Testament Ethics* (New York: HarperCollins, 1996), 309.

21. Ibid., 300.

22. Ogden, *Reality of God and Other Essays,* 210-11.

23. Identified as the primordial nature of God. Cobb and Griffin, *Process Theology,* 98.

24. Cobb, *Christ in a Pluralistic Age,* 169.

25. Ibid., 184. "The universal principle of life and light, creation and redemption, which is the presence of God in all things, is what we [Christians] call Christ" (Cobb, answering a question from Jeanyne B. Slettom, *Process Perspective,* 37).

26. Ibid., 169.

27. Ibid., 186.

28. Ibid., 187.

29. Ibid., 181-85.

30. Suchocki, *God, Christ, Church,* 90-92.

31. Marjorie Hewitt Suchocki, *Divinity and Diversity: A Christian Affirmation of Religious Pluralism* (Nashville: Abingdon Press, 2003), 46.

32. Suchocki, *God, Christ, Church,* 40-41.

33. Ibid., 170.

34. Ibid., 103.

35. Ibid., 97.

36. Ibid., 47.

37. "How we name God reflects the cultural traditions through which we have been formed or transformed, and each is true. Christians come to God through Jesus Christ just as Muslims come to God as Allah through Muhammad" (ibid., 52).

38. Suchocki, *God, Christ, Church*, 170-71.

39. Ibid., 216.

40. Ibid.

41. Ibid., 179. All routes to the divine harmony have a place in the "divine center," 216.

42. Suchocki, *Divinity and Diversity*, "A Theology of the reign of God calls us toward a new affirmation of religious pluralism," 82.

43. Ogden, *Reality of God and Other Essays*, 224.

44. Ibid., 226.

45. Ibid.

46. Ibid., 229.

47. Alfred North Whitehead said that his philosophy is "entirely neutral on the question of immortality, or on the existence of purely spiritual beings other than God," *Religion in the Making* (The Bronx, NY: Fordham Univ. Press, 1996), 111.

48. Ogden, *Reality of God and Other Essays*, 229-30.

49. Ibid., 211.

50. Cobb and Griffin, *Process Theology*, 123-24.

51. *Process Perspective*, 108. Cobb is willing to allow for the continuing existence of "primarily mental occasions after the death of the body," 106-7.

52. Cobb and Griffin, *Process Theology*, 121-23.

53. Marjorie Hewitt Suchocki, *The End of Evil: Process Eschatology in Historical Context* (Albany, NY: State Univ. of New York Press, 1988), 81-82. "Only if [our] partial triumphs over evil in history may be read as intimations of an order where all evil is everlastingly overcome is it legitimate to conceive of any full answer to evil, or of God as the final overcomer," 81.

54. Suchocki, *God, Christ, Church*, 205.

55. Ibid., 202. Suchocki's most extensive development of the hope of continued life after death is located in *End of Evil*, chapters V-VI. She develops key process concepts to provide "an adequate answer to evil." Her goal is a coherent theory of an ultimate overcoming of evil beyond our immediate experience of the world. Suchocki develops the idea of "subjective immortality," a concept not used by Whitehead but which "seems to haunt the edges of his system." She shows how a person might be "reborn to subjective immortality" (*End of Evil*, 82, 84, 96). By the time Suchocki concludes her creative effort, it becomes clear that by "resurrection" she means something far different from the Christian doctrine of resurrection that centers on the continuity and transformation of the whole individual person (1 Cor. 15). "We are discussing a metaphysics whereby occasions of experience, not substantial persons," are finally "created as a composite personality of God" (107, 108).

56. Suchocki, *God, Christ, Church*, 206.

57. Ibid., 202-3.

58. Ibid., 206.

59. Ibid., 229. Suchocki explains Father, Son, and Holy Spirit by exploring the concepts "presence, wisdom, and power." "God is trinity in presence, wisdom, and power in the dimensions of human experience" (229 ff.).

60. Suchocki, *End of Evil*, 112-13.

61. William Hasker warns that "when given excessive authority, so that it becomes the yardstick by which the gospel itself is measured, the Whiteheadian scheme can become a prison for theology" (William Hasker, "In Response to David Ray Griffin," in *Searching for an Adequate God: A Dialogue Between Process and Free Will Theists* [Grand Rapids: Eerdmans, 2000], 39-52).

Chapter 7

1. Suchocki, *God, Christ, Church.*
2. John Cobb is noteworthy in these efforts, with intensely practical reflections on the efficacy of prayer (*Prayer for Jennifer* [Eugene, OR: Wipf and Stock, 2000]); the battle with doubt (*Doubting Thomas: Christology in Story Form* [New York: Crossroad Publishing, 1990]); lay theology (*Lay Theology* [Atlanta: Chalice Press, 1994]); and other practical topics.
3. Cobb and Griffin, *Process Theology,* 113.
4. Ibid.
5. "What Is Process Thought?" Center for Process Studies, http://ctr4process.org/about/process/
6. Cobb and Griffin, *Process Theology,* 56.
7. David Ray Griffin: "Whitehead . . . did not believe that morality could be autonomous. Holding that our ideals and thereby our actions are inevitably shaped by our worldviews, he believed that if a society's worldview does not support morality, the society's moral life would inevitably deteriorate. Given the nature of the late modern worldview, therefore, he considered the overriding moral need of our time to be the development of a new morality-supporting cosmology" (*Reenchantment Without Supernaturalism,* 287).
8. Whitehead, *Process and Reality* (1978), 27.
9. Here I utilize the terminology from Thomas Jay Oord's chapter "The Love Racket" in *The Altruism Reader: Selections from Writings on Love, Religion and Science* (West Conshohocken, PA: Templeton Foundation Press, 2007), 23. Oord defines love: "agape is intentional response to promote overall well-being when confronted by that which generates ill-being."
10. Brian G. Henning, *The Ethics of Creativity: Beauty, Morality and Nature in a Processive Cosmos* (Pittsburgh: Univ. of Pittsburgh Press, 2005), 222.
11. Kevin Durand, *Sidgwick's Utility and Whitehead's Virtue: Metaphysics and Morality* (Lanham, MD: Univ. Press of America, 2002), 156. Durand points to James Gray, John Hick, and Richard Davis as thinkers who have expressed doubts about Whitehead's purported rejection of utilitarianism.
12. Whitehead, *Process and Reality* (1978), 355.

Chapter 9

1. It is in this respect the equivalent of a fading pop phenomenon. Although *Momma Mia!* may have been a commercial success in 2008, it in no way signals a comeback for the 1970s pop music group ABBA.
2. It has been intriguing to watch the "evangelistic" fervor of process theologians. I recall the delight in the Center for Process Studies, when it acquired some bumper stickers printed for an East Coast political candidate with just the right name. Their message captured the hopes and dreams of the center: "Another Household for Whitehead!" Yet apart from receiving some attention in the U.K., passing acknowledgment (and criticism) by a very few German theologians, and minimal recent attention by theologians interested in the French philosopher Gilles Deleuze, process philosophy has made little impact on theology outside Anglo-America and is hardly in the main current of early twenty-first-century theology.
3. Whitehead is not the only inspiration for process theology. It is possible to broaden the term to include approaches to theology inspired by a wide range of thinkers, including Hegel, Dilthey, Bergson, Dewey, Alexander, Teilhard, and others. However, Whitehead is quite dominant, often as interpreted by his former assistant, Charles Hartshorne. Because of the dominance of Whitehead, this chapter concentrates on his work.
4. He drew especially from Plato, Aristotle, and the Stoics.

Notes

5. He drew especially from Leibniz, Spinoza, Locke, Hume, and Kant. He drew as well from such late nineteenth- and early twentieth-century figures as Bergson, Bradley, James, and Dewey.

6. He considered the Old Testament view of God to be barbaric. The view of God and of human life he thought he had found in the New Testament is close to the vision of late-nineteenth-century Protestant liberalism. Whitehead's own designation for the God of his metaphysics is "the fellow sufferer who understands."

7. Whether Whiteheadian metaphysics is technically totalitarian is yet to be determined.

8. Alfred North Whitehead, *Process and Reality: An Essay in Cosmology—Corrected Edition*, eds. David Ray Griffin and Donald W. Sherburne (New York: Free Press, 1978), 7.

9. One adjustment Charles Hartshorne made to Whitehead's metaphysics is to imagine the cosmos as God's "body." Thus, to revere the universe is to revere the very body of God. God is most responsible for maintaining the order by which the world has enough coherence to be a body. Therefore, for Hartshorne one would best revere God only as one simultaneously reveres the cosmos and the manager who keeps it together. Still, no less for Hartshorne than for Whitehead, God and God's "body" are held tightly in the fist of laws that keep God in check no less than any other entity.

10. However, this God does give investment advice and is quite a competent business manager.

11. This is not to say that process theologians are quick to affirm such a thing. In fact, process theologians have expended considerable energy marketing their approach as "Christian." If pressed, process theologians are happy to redefine orthodox theological terms in order to make them conform to a Whiteheadian vision. This is perhaps their most infuriating strategy. My friend Warren Brown says that process theology turns words into "semantic mules." "Mules" are those desperate people who hire themselves out to carry contraband, for example, in their bellies to the far side of a closely watched border, where it is later unloaded. Process theologians routinely take ordinary theological terms and fill them with contents supplied by a Whiteheadian laboratory. At first it may appear that they are in agreement with the Scriptures or traditions of the church. Often no doubt they are. However, it is not unusual for them only to appear to be. Process theologians are not the only intellectuals who perform this maneuver, but they are the most blatant and persistent. In fact, I seldom leave a conversation with a process theologian without feeling that I have just escaped being conned.

12. Often, in fact, process theologians are quite critical of consumerism. One thinks of black pots and kettles.

13. And assimilate whatever intensity of feeling they obtained.

14. Process theology is blatantly Pelagian. "Grace" is initial guidance and enticement in the becoming of the moment *I am*. That is all. As a theology it is all but graceless.

15. Alfred North Whitehead, *Religion in the Making* (New York: World Publishing, 1954), 16. Compare this with the apostle Paul's exhortation to the Christians in Rome. They should, in love born of the Spirit, actually enter into the suffering or rejoicing spirit of another (Rom. 12:15).

16. As any number is divided by larger and larger numbers, it becomes progressively diminished in value. When divided by infinity, its value is zero. One moment in a vast universe over the course, say, of 14 billion years becomes relatively insignificant, when compared to the whole. However, if the universe never had a first moment, the number of moments that have already occurred is infinite. If the universe will never have had a last moment, it dissolves into an infinitely receding future.

17. On a macro scale.

Notes

18. Whitehead's designation for the retention of the remnants of the dead in the organic unity of God and of other living entities is "objective immortality." That is a nice poetic turn of phrase but is not to be confused with what came forth out of the garden tomb on Easter Sunday morning.

19. There are methodological problems with picking out and quoting short passages, especially from three different biblical books, one of which is by a different author. Nonetheless, on the point being argued in this paragraph, these texts seem to agree.

Chapter 10

1. The actual occasion receives its initial aim from God, but in its own free activity of becoming it adapts the aim to its own subjective choice of what it will actually become (Suchocki, *God, Christ, Church,* 39).

2. Cobb and Griffin, *Process Theology,* 27-29.

3. Cobb, *God and the World,* 83-94. Craig Keen says there is another way to look at this. There seems to be "a pretty good chance that the relative 'value' of such achievements will grow steadily less, as more and more 'value' is accumulated in God's physical pole" (conversation 9/4/09). Defenders of process thought say that unlike our human inability to preserve the past without diminishment, no value ever diminishes in God's consequent nature. I question whether process thought ever shows how this is metaphysically possible.

4. Suchocki, *God, Christ, Church,* 83.

5. Ibid., 188.

6. God as creative love is identified as the primordial nature of God. God's primordial nature is also identified with the Logos. Cobb and Griffin, *Process Theology,* 98.

7. Ibid., 48. A qualification needs to be added regarding God suffering with us. The late British theologian Colin Gunton points out that only in part of God's being does he suffer with others, namely, his *consequent* nature. God in his *primordial* nature does not suffer with the world, even though what happens in the world affects the aims God offers to the world (Gunton, *Becoming and Being* [1980], 21).

8. Suchocki, *God, Christ, Church,* 190.

9. Whitehead, *Process and Reality* (1978), 7, 21. "Creativity" is the first "Category of the Ultimate." It is the "universal of universals characterizing ultimate matter of fact. It is that ultimate principle by which the many, which are the universe disjunctively, become the one actual occasion, which is the universe conjunctively. . . . 'Creativity' is the principle of novelty. . . . The 'creative advance' is the application of this ultimate principle of creativity to each novel situation which it originates," 21).

10. Ibid., 7. An "accident" is any entity, event, or thing dependent upon or that expresses—even if imperfectly—a reality that transcends it. "Accidents" figure in traditional metaphysics as marking the distinction between an existing thing and the substance (essence) that underlies it.

11. Ibid., 20, 29, 43.

12. Ibid., 43.

13. Whitehead: "In all philosophical theory there is an ultimate which is actual in virtue of its accidents. It is only then capable of characterization through its accidental embodiments, and apart from these accidents is devoid of actuality. In the philosophy of organism [process philosophy] this ultimate is termed 'creativity'" (*Process and Reality* [1978], 7).

14. Ibid., 41.

15. God's *primordial* nature is the source from which every occasion of experience receives its initial aim. Cobb, *God and the World,* 83.

16. Charles Hartshorne, *Man's Vision of God and the Logic of Theism* (1941), as quoted by Colin Gunton, *Becoming and Being* (1978), 33.

17. Cobb, *God and the World*.
18. Colin Gunton makes this telling point. *Becoming and Being* (1980), 29. This is clearly true of Hartshorne. It may be only implicitly true of Whitehead. But unquestionably for both of them God is a constituent and contingent part of the whole. John Cobb says that since God is all-inclusive, "we are parts of God." But God is more than the sum total of the parts (*God and the World*, 79).
19. Karl Barth, *Church Dogmatics* II/1:310-11, eds. G. W. Bromily and T. F. Torrence (London: T & T Clark International, 2004).
20. Ben Witherington III, *The Indelible Image: The Theological and Ethical Thought World of the New Testament* (Downers Grove, IL: IVP Academic, 2009), 1:180-81.
21. William Stegall, "Perspective from Process Theology," The Center for Process Studies, http://ctr4process.org/about/process/GodUniverse.shtml.
22. Suchocki, *God, Christ, Church*, 70.
23. God's *primordial* nature is the source from which every occasion of experience receives its initial aim. Cobb, *God and the World*, 83.
24. Ibid.
25. Charles Hartshorne, *Man's Vision of God* (1941), as quoted by Gunton, *Becoming and Being* (1980), 33.
26. Suchocki, *God, Christ, Church*, 170.
27. Barth, *Church Dogmatics* II/2:19. At heart, process theology is at least semi-Pelagian, if not Pelagian outright.
28. Ibid., 27.
29. Jenson, *God After God*, 151.

Chapter 11

1. Witherington, *Indelible Image*, 1:203.
2. Ibid., 208.
3. Griffin, *Reenchantment Without Supernaturalism*, 68.
4. Suchocki, *End of Evil*, 68.
5. Ibid., 76.
6. Ibid., *Reenchantment Without Supernaturalism*, 213.
7. Ibid., 218.
8. David Ray Griffin, "Postmodern Animism and Life After Death," in *God and Religion in the Postmodern World* (Albany, NY: State Univ. of New York Press, 1989), 102. Griffin affirms this same sentiment in his chapter "Reconstructive Theology," in *The Cambridge Companion to Postmodern Theology*, ed. Kevin J. Vanhoozer (Cambridge: Cambridge Univ. Press, 2003), 104.
9. Griffin, *Reenchantment Without Supernaturalism*, 215.
10. Ibid., 230.
11. Whitehead, *Process and Reality* (1978), 351.
12. Charles Hartshorne, *Creative Synthesis and Philosophic Method* (LaSalle, IL: Open Court; London: SCM Press, 1970), 289.
13. Hartshorne, *Omnipotence and Other Theological Mistakes*, 117.
14. Suchocki, *End of Evil*, 185.
15. Suchocki, *God, Christ, Church*, 185.
16. Griffin, "Postmodern Animism," 96.
17. Witherington, *Indelible Image*, 1:238-39.
18. Griffin, *Reenchantment Without Supernaturalism*, 246.
19. Griffin, "Reconstructive Theology," 106.
20. Griffin, "Postmodern Animism," 102.

21. Suchocki, *End of Evil*, 81.
22. Ibid., 83.
23. Ibid., 155.

Chapter 13

1. John Wesley, "On Divine Providence," Sermon 67 in *The Works of John Wesley* (Nashville: Abingdon, 1985), 2:541.

2. John Calvin says, for instance, "Adam did not fall without the ordination and will of God. It offends the ears of some when it is said that God willed this fall. But what else is the permission of Him who has the power of preventing and in whose hand the whole matter is placed but his will?" *Commentaries on the First Book of Moses Called Genesis*, vol. 1 (Christian Classics Ethereal Library, Grand Rapids), http://www.ccel.org (accessed Nov. 25, 2009).

3. John Wesley, "Upon our Lord's Sermon on the Mount, III," Sermon 23 in *The Works of John Wesley* (Nashville: Abingdon, 1984), 1:519.

4. Randy L. Maddox, *Responsible Grace: John Wesley's Practical Theology* (Nashville: Kingswood, 1994), 36.

Conclusion

1. John Dillenberger, ed., *Martin Luther: Selections from His Writings* (Garden City, N.Y.: Anchor Books, 1961), 270.

2. Luke Timothy Johnson, *The Writings of the New Testament: an Interpretation* (Norwich, UK: SCM Press, 2003).

3. N. T. Wright, *The Challenge of Jesus* (London: SPCK Publishing, 2000).

4. Karl Barth, *Dogmatics in Outline* (Norwich, UK: SCM Press, 2001).

Appendix A

1. Whitehead, *Process and Reality* (1978), 22.
2. Ibid., 22.
3. Ibid., 23.
4. Ibid., 21.
5. Ibid.
6. Ibid., 7.
7. Ibid.
8. Ibid., 23.
9. Ibid., 7.
10. Ibid.
11. Ibid., 29.
12. Suchocki, *God, Christ, Church*, 258-59.
13. Whitehead, *Process and Reality* (1978), 23.
14. Ibid., 22.
15. http://ctr4process.org/about/process/
16. Ibid., 8.
17. Cobb and Griffin, *Process Theology*, 15.
18. Ibid., 28.

www.ingramcontent.com/pod-product-compliance
Lightning Source LLC
Chambersburg PA
CBHW070148100426
42743CB00013B/2854